THE
SAVOY
FOOD AND DRINK BOOK

THE ROYAL ENG... ...OPERA

SAVOY... ...THEATRE

Vincent Brooks Day & Son Lith.

"Royal English Opera."

RICHARD D'OYLY CARTE

THE
SAVOY
FOOD AND DRINK BOOK

EDITED BY ALISON LEACH

SALEM HOUSE PUBLISHERS
Massachusetts Topsfield

EDITOR: ALISON LEACH
PHOTOGRAPHY: PETER WILLIAMS
CONSULTANT ART DIRECTOR: RAYMOND HAWKEY
DESIGNERS: CHRISTOS KONDEATIS AND ROY TREVELION
COOKERY CONSULTANT: JANE SUTHERING
U.S. RECIPE CONSULTANT: BEVERLY LE BLANC

Salem House is honored to be the publisher of *The Savoy Food and Drink Book.* The recipes in this edition have been carefully adapted for American usage. Supplementary sections on garnishes, sauces, food preparation techniques and culinary terms explain how to prepare these dishes to the high standards of The Savoy kitchens.

First published in the United States 1988 by
Salem House Publishers 462 Boston Street Topsfield MA 01983

Designed and produced by Genesis Productions Limited
30 Great Portland Street London W1N 5AD

Library of Congress Cataloging-in-Publication Data:

The Savoy food and drink book/edited by Alison Leach
224pp 26.7cm x 20cm
Includes index
ISBN 0-88162-374-1: $29.95
1. Cookery, International. 2. Beverages. 3. Savoy Hotel (London,
England) – History. I. Leach, Alison.
TX725.A1S38 1988 641.5 – dc19 88-336

Color separations by Val Haven Limited, London
Printed and bound in Spain by Cayfosa Industria Gráfica S.A., Barcelona

CONTENTS

LINCOLN TABER'S TROMPE L'OEIL MURAL IN THE
THAMES FOYER

INTRODUCTION

The folk-lore I imbibed about The Savoy as a lad in the thirties said of course that it was grand and sumptuous, but in a quiet, reserved sort of way, not flashy or foreign or frequented by the mysterious adventuresses' I was reading about in the works of Sapper and Dornford Yates. When my father mentioned The Savoy, which admittedly was not all that often, it was always in tones of great respect. This may have been something to do with the fact that he was a terrific Gilbert and Sullivan fan, like all the family (except me). But anyway, The Savoy was one of those unique places that made London what it was and would always be there, like Big Ben, St Paul's, Lord's cricket ground and, not a mile off along the Embankment, my father's school and mine, the City of London.

In the long years when my idea of a large evening out was dinner for two at Morgan's Tudor Grill, Swansea, I had few chances to check my early impressions of The Savoy. But times changed, I became an author and was summoned in due course to be regaled by my publisher, the illustrious Victor Gollancz, at the Savoy Restaurant, where he was said to have lunch *every day*. This seemed to me an almost ridiculously high level on which to be living, one that brought some risk of becoming over-stuffed with luxuries, though it was a risk I personally might have considered taking at the time, given the chance. Of course I know better now.

Up I turned on the dot and was taken straight to the great man's regular table by the window – no time-wasting nonsense in bar or lounge before going in. Nor was any apéritif mentioned when I had settled myself. (It was not our first meeting.) Quite soon, in fact, Victor was studying the menu.

'I think tomato salad sounds the sort of thing to go for, don't you?' he said. 'It's always good here.'

'Oh, fine with me.'

'And then the chef does a very nice steak-and-kidney pie on Thursdays.'

'Does he now?'

I reasoned that today must be Thursday or Victor would probably not have bothered to mention that pie. I also reasoned that not only had I not yet been allowed a peep at a menu but that I was never going to see one if I sat there till tea-time. This ploy was new to me and I like to think I had the waiter's sympathy, but there was nothing to be done by either of us.

'And I don't know about you,' said my host, 'but I'm going to have some beer.'

Old Victor Gollancz was famous for his great way with the English language but even he never came up with anything more brilliant than that last remark. The steak-and-kidney pie turned out to be delicious, I remember, and the beer suited me down to the ground. Nevertheless I must have promised myself there and then that my future relations with The Savoy were not going to be on those lines.

Everything was as different as could be on the day in 1984 when I went down there to attend the lunch to celebrate Eric Ambler's 75th birthday. I had come straight from the memorial service in Westminster Abbey for an old friend, John Betjeman, and I needed good company and good cheer. They were there in plenty in the Patience Room. Ambler, the man who by universal consent invented the modern spy thriller, was being honoured by a gathering of thriller writers of more recent vintage: Anthony Price, Gavin Lyall, John le Carré, H. R. F. Keating, John Gardner, Frederick Forsyth, Julian Symons, Len Deighton, Lionel Davidson, Miles Tripp, Ted Allbeury. I sneaked in as the pseudonymous author of a one-off James Bond pastiche, and I felt I too was being honoured in a smaller way by being invited.

Far from immediately, we sat down to eat – we would have been thirteen at table but for The Savoy tradition of adding Kaspar to the company in such circumstances. Kaspar is a large doll in catlike form, rather horrifyingly appropriate, I thought, among chroniclers of dark and fearful deeds. He had little to say but everyone else had a lot. All of us made speeches, some of us in instalments. In one of mine I toasted everybody present, saying enthusiastically but truthfully that at different times each of them had added to my pleasure in life, also saying no less truthfully but more plaintively that I could think of no other assemblage in the world – certainly not a bunch of poets, for instance – where I could have said as much. More speeches and refreshment followed. Finally, in an operation as skilful as any in his novels, Len Deighton picked up the bill and made his getaway unseen.

It must have been later, not then, that I reviewed the occasion more objectively. The way the whole deal had been handled, the absence of the fuss-plus-muddle I had thought was inevitable at functions in private rooms, the feeling that you were completely secluded and yet could be brought anything you wanted in five seconds – well, it all showed me what was *possible*. And it was grand enough without either servility or condescension, something a boy from south of the river never forgets to appreciate.

A couple of years later, having come some distance from those early Gollancz days, I managed to win the Booker Prize for Fiction with my novel *The Old Devils*. Winning a thing like that, you know, is not like winning the 1000 metres at Wembley: it is no less exhausting but it takes much, much longer to happen. The first stage came when I was signing copies at a bookshop in Covent Garden and was urgently summoned to the telephone – I was on the short list! By what felt like an inevitable process, a law of nature, I found myself a few seconds afterwards, in the presence of a contingent from my publishers, drinking a large Dry Martini in the cocktail bar of The Savoy. This venue was already well known to me as a good place to entertain pretty young American graduate students. Later that evening and far from where I had started I was promised a lift home by a new acquaintance, a very merry fellow who kept saying we would be off just as soon as he had had another drink. No alternative seemed feasible. Growing alarm had begun to sober me up when he produced a Mercedes with a liveried chauffeur in it.

When the time came, and much to my permanent gratitude and satisfaction and the relief of those responsible for my finances, I finally and irreversibly won the Booker. My publishers had served me well enough, and been nice enough to me, for me to consider I owed them something. I further considered I owed myself something for the ceremonial dinner I had been unable to eat for all sorts of reasons, one of which was that it was uneatable. (Not that I would hold that against anybody faced with the task of serving up a full-dress meal for a couple of hundred in the vast, chilly Guildhall.) As before, what more natural and inevitable than a little private lunch at The Savoy? A handy rendezvous for my publishers from their offices in Chandos Place, sure, but that was not going to cut any ice with me, to whom anywhere in London or most of the Home Counties would have been handy that day, and whose treat was it? No, it *had* to be The Savoy.

Not many people will be surprised to learn that my memory of the occasion is not detailed. We assembled in the Iolanthe Room and from beginning to end the whole show went swimmingly. There was smoked salmon and a very good rack of lamb, there was a great deal of champagne and a certain amount of claret and not a little vintage port. And there was probably quite a lot of vaunting, vainglorious talk, led by me. Almost certainly I quoted an aphorism of that hoary old American novelist, Gore Vidal: 'It is not enough to succeed; others must fail,' – well, it was our day. I am quite positive we agreed that, when I get my dukedom or am appointed Archbishop of Canterbury, whichever comes first, we will reconvene, and in the self-same place.

After all, where else is there?

KINGSLEY AMIS

THE SAVOY HOTEL.

AN ENGRAVING FROM THE 'ILLUSTRATED LONDON NEWS' OF 1889

ONE HUNDRED GLORIOUS YEARS

Like all great institutions, The Savoy has a motto. In the early days, it was *Noscitur a sociis* – literally 'It is recognised among friends', perhaps better rendered as 'Birds of a feather flock together'. Since the Second World War the motto has been 'For Excellence We Strive', one of those stirring slogans we old cynics forget as soon as we read it. But in the service area behind the great banqueting rooms, where muted bustle provides unobtrusive service to hundreds of diners, there is a hand-lettered sign stuck up above a doorway, not by the management but by an ordinary member of staff. It simply says:

REMEMBER: For EXCELLENCE we STRIVE.

There are luxury hotels competing with each other in every country, but there is only one Savoy, the *ne plus ultra*. None other has sustained the steady excellence of The Savoy over a century.

This site on the King's Reach of the Thames, on the bend of the river, has been entertaining travellers for a thousand years, some more willing than others. In 1246 Henry III presented the land, then between the two cities of London and Westminster, to his wife's uncle Peter of Savoy, who had followed Eleanor to England to see what pickings were to be had from her fortunate marriage. The ancient Duchy of Savoy, now divided between France, Switzerland and Italy, had many links with Britain, and the part of London where Peter built his great palace was soon called 'Soffey', or Savoy.

Peter entertained prodigally; perhaps his statue is placed above the stainless steel canopy of the Strand

THE FAMILIAR STRAND ENTRANCE TO THE SAVOY

entrance to the hotel as an inspiration to the staff. He went off to recapture Turin from Charles I of Naples in 1266, and was made Prince of Savoy two years later.

The Palace subsequently became the residence of John of Gaunt, Duke of Lancaster, before being burnt down in 1381 during Wat Tyler's insurrection. Still the property of the Duchy of Lancaster, it lay in ruins for a hundred years before a hospice was built on the site. In the seventeenth century the hospice was run by the Jesuits. In the eighteenth century the area became an early example of urban blight and inner

ENGAGING ROOMS BY MARCONIGRAM

city decay; a haunt of thieves, footpads and prostitutes. It was still largely derelict by the time Richard D'Oyly Carte came to build his triumphantly innovative Savoy Theatre in 1881.

Richard D'Oyly Carte was the genius behind The Savoy Hotel. He was primarily a theatrical impresario, the Cameron Mackintosh of his day with Gilbert and Sullivan as his Rice and Lloyd Webber. The trio first collaborated in 1875, achieving instant success, and by 1880 they were making a phenomenal profit of

£60,000 a year. D'Oyly Carte invested his share in the building of the Savoy Theatre, where as well as having the first public building in the world boasting electric lights, he was credited with inventing the queue in order to control the crowds of people trying to get tickets. The invention was successfully exported to countries such as Russia and Poland, but it met with less enthusiasm in France and Italy.

D'Oyly Carte had the Midas touch. With a massive cash surplus, he thought at first of building a block of flats on the rest of the Savoy site, then decided on an hotel. Work began in 1884, and the hotel took five years to build. Looking back from the safety of a hundred years it is difficult for us to grasp how revolutionary the entire concept and execution were.

Thomas Collcutt, who at the same time was designing a huge folly tower at the Imperial Institute in South Kensington, was commissioned as the architect, although Arthur Mackmurdo, who designed the interiors, was originally credited with the work. Architecturally The Savoy was unprecedented. Seven storeys high, it was the first steel-framed building in London as well as the first to use concrete in its construction. Electricity was supplied by its own generating station in the basement and it even had a private artesian well supplying soft water, an unheard-of luxury in London.

D'Oyly Carte demanded perfection. Conscious of the embarrassment of tipping, he also introduced an all-in tariff, with no hidden extras. No Fees! was his slogan in theatre and hotel, and because of The Savoy's modernity he could abolish, as a visiting American approvingly wrote, 'the old hotel notion of extracting payment for the three necessaries of life – baths, lights and attendance'. Two years earlier the Hotel Victoria in Northumberland Avenue had opened in a blaze of publicity with no fewer than four bathrooms between its five hundred guests. The Savoy had seventy bathrooms.

A few hotels in America already had lifts, although they were still very much a novelty, but those at The Savoy were no mere lifts. They were Ascending Rooms, built by the American Elevator Company; spacious, luxurious and panelled in Japanese red lacquer. Lifts meant more profit to the hotelier; previously the more stairs one had to climb, the cheaper

GEORGES AUGUSTE ESCOFFIER

SOUVENIR OF A SUPPER CELEBRATING PUCCINI'S NEW
OPERA MADAM BUTTERFLY AT COVENT GARDEN

the rooms became. An 1893 sales brochure for the hotel tried to put this revolutionary new concept across:

'The hotel is designed to embrace suites of rooms, each suite compact, comfortable and complete in itself. A suite comprises a private sitting room, or rooms, one or more private bedrooms, a private bathroom, lavatory etc. Each set is thus a little home in itself. Those nearest the sky are just as spacious and lofty as those on the ground floor. That is why the charge is the same for a set just under the roof.'

In August 1889 The Savoy opened. London came, and stared, and wondered, and went away again. The hotel was glorious, opulent, magnificent, but it lacked character. D'Oyly Carte recognised the problem: his manager, Mr Hardwicke, did not have the necessary

charisma. He also knew how to solve it and in 1888 he had made an approach to César Ritz, the prince of hoteliers, to ask him to manage the new Savoy. Ritz elegantly declined, preferring the leisured ambience of the resort hotels he had run in Monte Carlo, Baden Baden, Lucerne and San Remo to what he regarded as the cold Calvinistic commercialism of London, at that time the most important city in the world but certainly no tourist centre.

Ritz knew instinctively how to flatter the nobility and the *haut monde* of his time, but like all supreme practitioners of the art of flattery he had no real defence against it when he was the object. D'Oyly Carte tempted him to London to stay in The Savoy as a guest for its opening, on an equal footing with real princes and maharajahs. There he was, this son of a Swiss shepherd from Niederwald, being treated as if he were royalty himself! And like a shepherd's son, he stared at riches unseen before. Never in a life well accustomed to the visual display of affluence had he seen such ostentatious prosperity. Nor was D'Oyly Carte's offer of a lump sum equal to his own annual salary an unacceptable incentive for his advice.

'The wealth and brilliance of London are simply indescribable,' wrote Ritz. London was booming. Incessantly, he began to make notes as to how this aspect of the hotel could be bettered, how that particular service could be improved, how the new-fangled electric light could be shaded to be more flattering to the lady guests, how the cooking by Chef Carpentier in general could never match the standard of one chef in particular. He was lost. The Savoy had claimed him as her own, and D'Oyly Carte had won his most treasured prize, the most renowned hotelier in the world.

Ritz went back briefly to his hotel in Cannes, agog with excitement, before returning to The Savoy. As D'Oyly Carte had anticipated, Ritz brought Autour as his assistant; Agostini as cashier; Echenard, a master of wine, as *maître d'hôtel*; and, of course, Auguste Escoffier, indisputably the world's greatest chef. The arrival of Ritz and Escoffier crowned the glory of The Savoy: within its first year it was recognised as the standard for all hotels to emulate.

Ritz and Escoffier had worked together since 1883, after Ritz had lost his current chef Jean Giroix to another hotel while managing the Grand Hotel Monte Carlo. Like D'Oyly Carte, he knew exactly what he wanted, and acting on Giroix's recommendation he had immediately telegraphed Escoffier to come and join him in Monte Carlo. Together they had created a new style at the Grand, effectively devising the conventions of today's international hotels. Escoffier introduced the *à la carte* menu; waiters were to wear white ties and aprons, station head waiters black ties, and Restaurant Managers morning coats. Nowadays it is all too familiar; then it was an astonishing novelty, the *dernier cri*.

When they came to The Savoy, Britain was regarded as a barbaric outpost in the world of gastronomy. This was partly due to the licensing laws which, although different, were as peculiar then as they are today, and partly due to the dictates of

society. It was not done for a lady to be seen dining in a public place, so hotels and restaurants catered for the gruffer and less refined palates of men, who were more likely to appreciate a healthy faceful of cigar smoke with their 'eternal joints and beefsteaks, boiled fowl with oyster sauce and apple tart' which formed the standard menu of the day.

Escoffier made no secret of the fact that he enjoyed cooking for women, so Ritz set out to alter the custom

THE FRONT COVER OF THE JULY 1906 ISSUE OF 'THE GENTLEWOMAN' DEPICTS THE NEW POPULARITY OF DINING OUT

of centuries. Not only did he succeed in an astonishingly short space of time, he also managed to change British law. With the help of allies and society leaders such as Lady de Grey and Mrs Keppel, it became fashionable for women to frequent The Savoy and subsequently other top class hotels and restaurants.

When the Prince of Wales, later Edward VII, dined at The Savoy with Mrs Langtry it was the ultimate recommendation. As friends of Ritz, Lily Langtry, Lord Randolph Churchill and others lobbied strongly for a change in the licensing laws, which at the time meant that restaurants had to close at 11.00 pm during the week and all day on Sunday. Soon The Savoy Restaurant was open till half past twelve and on Sundays too.

Perhaps this, more than anything, was Ritz's great achievement at The Savoy, in that he changed an entrenched attitude in London society, a society notoriously resistant to change. People began to feel that not only was it socially acceptable to dine at The Savoy, but that it was smarter than dining at home. Nineteen hundred years after the Roman invasion the *passeggio* came to London.

With the passage of time, the name Escoffier has come to sound remote and Olympian, as the great chef has acquired legendary status. Yet the man

himself was warm, generous and approachable, modest and restrained in his habits. Like Ritz, he came from peasant stock – he was the son of a blacksmith in Provence – but unlike Ritz, he never acquired a cosmopolitan veneer. Even after ten years in England he could only speak a few words of the language, and was at his happiest when in control of his beloved kitchens. Oddly enough he rarely tasted the dishes he prepared, relying on his remarkable well-developed sense of smell.

Escoffier's true genius lay in his inventiveness. London had never seen or tasted food like his before: *Soufflé d'Ecrevisses à la Florentine; Brochettes d'Ortolan; Pêches à l'Orientale; Canard en Chemise.* All these classic dishes, originated by Escoffier, testify to the man's brilliance. While his talent was acclaimed throughout his working life, his contemporaries esteemed him more for the composition of his menus than for individual dishes.

'Very few people,' wrote Escoffier, 'know what an

THE SUPPER CROWD AT THE SAVOY ARE ENTERTAINED BY
AN EXHIBITION OF THE TANGO

THE FAMOUS
SUPPER SCENE
at
THE SAVOY

At the close of the play—
when notable members
of the dramatic world
and their audiences alike
transfer their thoughts to
the Hotel and Restaurant
—is the moment when
the suggestion of Supper
at the Savoy asserts itself.

Few of the novelties
which have from time to
time swayed the world of
fashion have had more
instant appeal than the
"Tango." Exhibitions of
the facinating innovation
graced many a brilliant
gathering drawn from
both behind and before
the footlights.

arduous task the composing of a perfect menu represents.' Here is one of his menus, from a dinner attended by European royalty on 25th June 1895:

Cantaloup
Consommé à la Française
Velouté à l'Italienne
Truite Saumonée Royale
Paupiettes de Sole aux Fines Herbes
Selle de Pré-salé aux Laitues
Petits Pois Bonne Femme
Suprêmes de Volaille Montpensier
Mousseline à l'Anglaise
Sorbet au Clicquot Rosé
Cailles aux Feuilles de Vigne
Brochettes d'Ortolans
Salade Alexandra
Soufflé d'Ecrevisses à la Florentine
Fonds d'Artichauts à la Moëlle
Pêches Princesse
Biscuit Glacé Savoy
Mignardises
Raisins. Nectarines

Escoffier was also past master at inventing dishes for the many glittering stars who frequented the hotel during the *belle époque*: a brilliant concept which flattered the guest as well as adding glamour and mystique to the dish. He created *Soufflé Tetrazzini* for Luisa Tetrazzini, *Mousseline de Volaille Patti* for Adelina Patti (who was managed by D'Oyly Carte) and, most famously of all, numerous dishes for the great Australian singer Dame Nellie Melba, who actually lived in the hotel for a year.

Sometimes these dishes commemorated particular performances: *Poularde Tosca*, for example, and *Pêches Melba*, originally dreamed up to cap a dinner to celebrate Dame Nellie's performance in *Lohengrin*. *Pêches au Cygne*, as it was first known, was a superb creation: fresh ripe peaches set on a bed of pure vanilla ice-cream, presented on the back of a great swan carved out of a single block of ice and covered with *sucre filé*. It was when Escoffier topped it with a *coulis de framboises* that it became known as *Pêches Melba*. Today, of course, the concoction universally known as Peach Melba – which too often means peaches with ice-

cream and raspberry jam – is a travesty of Escoffier's creation. His actual recipe reads as follows:

'Poach the peaches in vanilla flavoured syrup. Dish them in a timbale upon a layer of vanilla ice-cream, and coat them with a raspberry purée.'

Then there was Melba toast, widely believed to be yet another Escoffier invention for Australia's queen

PROFESSIONAL DANCERS DEMONSTRATE THE LATEST
BALLROOM DANCING STEPS

of song: but this was, in truth, a Savoy creation. Madame Ritz inspired it, Ritz suggested the method, Escoffier produced it and called it 'toast Marie' after Madame Ritz – but she modestly passed the honour to Dame Nellie.

For the Prince of Wales, Escoffier devised the extravagantly named *Cuisses de Nymphes à l'Aurore* – Thighs of Dawn Nymphs, in Shakespeare's tongue. The brou-haha when the 'dawn nymphs' proved to be frogs was deafening, but such was the power that the Prince's whims had on society that the following year more frogs' legs were consumed in London than in Paris. Here is the recipe:

'Poach the frogs' legs in an excellent white wine court-bouillon. *When cooled, trim them properly, dry them in a piece of fine linen, and steep them, one after the other, in a* chaud-froid *sauce of fish with paprika, the tint of which*

Untypically for a Frenchman, Escoffier added that frogs were 'the pet abomination of all classes of the population'.

There were equally impressive recipes such as *Pêches au Château Lafite* (simpler, too – 'poach the peaches in sufficient Château Lafite to cover them') which, even if you were to use a cooking vintage of Lafite like 1977, would now cost you in the region of £20 worth of wine for each peach. His recipe for *Truffes à la Crème* begins, 'Take 1 lb of truffles. . .'. Truffles today sell in the market at Riberac for £225 a

THE SAVOY ORPHEANS IN THE TWENTIES

should be golden. This done, arrange the treated legs on a layer of champagne jelly, which should have set beforehand on the bottom of a square, silver dish or crystal bowl. Now lay some chervil pluches *and tarragon leaves between the legs in imitation of water-grasses, and cover the whole with champagne jelly to counterfeit the effect of water. Send the dish to the table, set in a block of ice, fashioned as fancy may suggest.'*

kilo, a far cry from Escoffier's days as a conscript at the siege of Metz in the Franco-Prussian war when he noted that truffles were easier to come by than potatoes.

As his wife was not an Anglophile and had not accompanied him to England, Escoffier lived alone at the hotel and poured all his energies into his work. A typical day went as follows:

6.30	Rise, and dress in a severely tailored frock coat. (The chef's toque was only worn on Sundays)
7.00	Inspect the kitchens
8.00	To the office to order food from Covent Garden and Les Halles. Prepare the day's menu. Breakfast in office
9.00	Work in the kitchens. (There was a strict no smoking and no drinking rule)
11.00	To the restaurant to talk with the manager and waiters, to receive and supply details of guests' preferences and dislikes
12.00	Lunch with César Ritz
1.00	To the kitchens
3.30	Office work
4.30	A rapid constitutional; perhaps the chance to visit some suppliers
6.00	Back to the kitchens
9.00	A light solitary dinner
10.00	To the office to write articles and books, and to prepare new menus
12.00	Final tour of the kitchens
00.30	Retire

On Escoffier's instructions, the leftovers from the Restaurant were given to the Poor Sisters of Charity and received by them gratefully; such a gesture would nowadays be considered hopelessly patronising and probably unhygienic to boot.

By the end of the century The Savoy was the world's pre-eminent hotel. It was the focus of London society, then the most glittering anywhere, the place to see and be seen. The cream of Europe and America passed through the white tiled courtyard: royalty and British aristocracy from the Prince of Wales to Lord de Grey and Lord Rosebery; American commercial princes like Vanderbilt and Organ; great European names such as Rothschild and Radziwill, Crespi and Castellane. Monet painted his series of views of the Thames from his room on the fifth floor.

Then in 1897, at the crest of the wave, Ritz resigned. For a lesser hotel it would have been a disaster; The Savoy scarcely faltered, despite the Prince of Wales's much publicised statement 'Where Ritz goes, I go'. The pretext was trifling – a long simmering feud with the housekeeper, Mrs Willis, had boiled into open hostility culminating in Ritz's sudden departure. With him, despite his pleas for them to stay, went his faithful team – including Escoffier.

D'Oyly Carte appeared to face a crisis, but once again his quest for perfection resulted in the ideal successor. No-one else could ever have the charisma of Ritz, but he had floated on an ocean of serenity, buoyed up by his intimates, and outside the charmed

circle, staff turnover was depressingly high. What was needed was not a carbon copy of Ritz, but a new style of management where the ego of the hotelier was subordinate to that of his guests.

D'Oyly Carte knew whom he wanted, but as so often happens the people most in demand were the people most reluctant to move. He bought the Restaurant Marivaux in Paris, and with it Thouraud the chef, and Joseph *le patron*. For a short time they made a team as formidable as Escoffier and Ritz though the style, of course, was different. Whereas Ritz might

GRILL

Couvert, 6d

Steak	...	...	1/6
Filet Steak	...	...	2/-
Mixed Grill	...	...	2/6
Grilled and Devilled Bone	...	...	1/6
Sole	...	2/-	3/-
Mutton Chop	...	...	1/6
Pork Chop	...	...	1/6
Mutton Cutlet (1)	...	...	1/-
Lamb Cutlets (2)	...	...	1/6
Kidneys (2)	...	...	1/-
Sausages (2)	...	...	1/-
Rasher of Bacon	...	...	1/-
Pigeon	...	...	3/6
Poulet	...	...from	7/-
Lobster (half)	...	...	2/6

GAME, ACCORDING TO SEASON'S PRICE.

Cold Lobster (according to size)	...		—
Lobster Salad	...	...	2/6
Chicken Mayonnaise	...	...	3/-
Welsh Rarebit	...	...	1/-
Scotch Woodcock	...	...	1/-

Mushrooms 1/-   Baked Potatoes 6d. each.
Tomatoes ... 9d.

AN EXTRACT FROM A SUPPER MENU FOR THE SAVOY
RESTAURANT IN FEBRUARY 1914

nowadays be regarded as an obsequious snob, Joseph (who, as a Frenchman, always carried a smouldering resentment of his parents for letting him be born in Birmingham) had an altogether more modern approach, and was not above making gentle fun of his high class guests. There is the story of a judge who, on being helped into his coat by Joseph, asked 'How d'ye know it's mine?' 'I don't, milord,' bowed Joseph, a little lower than usual, 'but you gave it to me.'

D'Oyly Carte was in a mood for expansion. With the acquisition of Claridge's in 1893, and the subsequent formation of The Savoy Group, he was looking for a managing director. The perfect candidate was one George Reeves-Smith, then working at the Berkeley, but there was a drawback: he was reluctant to leave. So in 1899 D'Oyly Carte simply bought the Berkeley, and a new captain came on board ship.

George Reeves-Smith, a Yorkshireman, had once

of the copyright of Gilbert and Sullivan productions, widely pirated in that country. He made the most of his time there by staying in the very best hotels and observing the way in which they were run. His plan was to emulate high American standards in Britain with a view to attracting American visitors to his own hotels and making them feel at home there. Never was this policy more fully vindicated than in his creation of the American Bar. When Prohibition was in force in the United States Americans visiting London flocked to The Savoy.

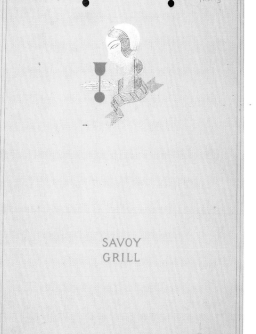

SAVOY
GRILL

SAVOY
RESTAURANT

worked as personal assistant to Jean Calvet, the celebrated 'King of Vintners' in Bordeaux, and was acknowledged to be a master of wine when D'Oyly Carte brought him in; but it was not for that quality that he was required. D'Oyly Carte saw in him the administrative flair that the Group would need to maintain its leadership. Although Reeves-Smith was forty when he started at The Savoy, he was to remain at the helm for the next forty years, receiving a knighthood towards the end of his illustrious career.

––––––––––

D'Oyly Carte was an inveterate traveller, particularly to the United States, which he often visited in defence

Harry Craddock, the world's most famous bartender and inventor of the famous White Lady cocktail, presided over the American Bar. Amazingly, Craddock himself was a teetotaller: did he know how good his drinks were? At the very suggestion of a special occasion he would devise a brand new cocktail to mark the event, a custom which The Savoy continues to this day under the direction of the head barman, Peter Dorelli.

Another feature of the American Bar, much appreciated by transatlantic visitors, was its understanding of how Americans like their drinks. Over here we fill the glass with drink, then add ice; over there they fill the glass with ice, then add the drink. It is a simple but

DECEMBER 11th, 1931.

THIRTIES GRAPHICS FROM THE SAVOY ARCHIVES

fundamental difference. The Savoy has always been one of the few establishments in Britain to understand how much ice Americans need in their drinks.

You could say that Harry Craddock effectively ushered in the cocktail age. Before he retired he put his most celebrated concoctions together into a book which became the definitive work on the subject. Early editions of the *Savoy Cocktail Book*, with its jazzy Gilbert Rumbold design epitomising the era, are now highly treasured. The title page describes the work as

> BEING in the main a complete compendium of the Cocktails, Rickeys, Daisies, Slings, Shrubs, Smashes, Fizzes, Juleps, Cobblers, Fixes and other Drinks, known and vastly appreciated in this year of grace 1930, with sundry notes of amusement and interest concerning them, together with subtle Observations upon Wines and their special occasions. BEING in the particular an elucidation of the Manners and Customs of people of quality in a period of some equality.

The book is a gem, with every conceivable kind of cocktail described, and laced with comments drier than a Savoy martini. 'Ladies are advised to avoid this Cocktail as often as possible' is typical of the tome's tone. The Loudspeaker Cocktail 'gives to Radio Announcers their peculiar enunciation. Three of them will produce oscillation, and after five it is possible to reach to osculation stage'. Instructions for the Thunderclap Cocktail are specific: 'Serve, then run for your life!' To the Corpse Reviver (a popular hangover cure) Craddock added the caveat, 'Four of these taken in swift succession will unrevive the corpse again', while the Earthquake Cocktail is 'so-called because if

there should happen to be an earthquake on while you are drinking it, it won't matter'.

After the horrors of the Great War those who were left behind played harder, a bright brittle counterpart to the dull muddy thump of the cannon. In the age of the 'flapper' and the Charleston novelty seemed a justification in itself, and no excuse was needed for the most outrageous behaviour or enterprise. Music, and particularly the wireless, was all the rage, and the BBC's predecessor, known as '2LO' gave its first broadcasts from Savoy Hill. The music they played was the sound of the Savoy Orpheans, the hotel's resident band.

Dining to music had for long been an established tradition at The Savoy: the ever-innovative Ritz had started the trend by hiring Johann Strauss, at a phenomenal fee, to 'cover the silence which hangs like a pall over an English dining table'. The habit reached its apogee with the Savoy Orpheans who, at the peak of their popularity in 1924, had a radio audience of 122 million throughout Europe; they were also picked up, via relay stations, across America and even in the Pacific. In the first ten months of their existence, they sold three million gramophone records, at a time when few people possessed the machines on which to play them.

The Savoy Orpheans claimed to be the first international all-star band, and the hotel publicity proudly announced:

'To obtain these ''stars'' 110,000 miles of fruitless journeys were made in searching for and bringing musicians from many parts of Europe and America – several coming from the Pacific coast – for tests and rehearsals.'

The Orpheans described their music as 'symphonised syncopation', and on their first anniversary received messages of congratulations from countless distinguished figures, amongst them Stokowski, Chaliapin and Arnold Bennett. Nearly half a century before we were dazzled by the light shows of Pink Floyd and other mega-bands, the Orpheans were offering fragments of Dvorak's New World Symphony 'with an orchestration of chromatic lighting'.

The Savoy ran several bands in the dancing years – Rudy Vallee joined the Savoy Havana Band in 1924, and in 1926 the popular Carroll Gibbons became leader of the Savoy Sylvians. Gibbons was a prodigiously talented pianist who studied at the Boston Conservatory and gave his first concert at the age of ten; apart from a few short breaks to run HMV's light music division and as MGM's composer in Hollywood, he remained at The Savoy till his tragically early death at the age of 51.

During the twenties and thirties, the *maître-chef* in The Savoy's main restaurant was the Frenchman François Latry, who had come from Claridge's in 1919 (he eventually retired in 1942). Latry coped superbly with the hectic fads and fashions of food through these two troubled decades, and his classic French cuisine had great appeal for American movie stars and British thespians alike – although neither group was averse to teasing the monoglot chef. Asked how he'd like his steak, Tex Austin, the rodeo impresario, drawled: 'Get a bullock, wound it slightly, and drive it in. . .' Bud Flanagan, on being served with a quiche, quipped 'Not Flan again!'

If they preferred, guests could eat in the Grill Room, a quite separate establishment with its own distinct identity. Taking as its motto 'Savoy-fare is savoir-vivre' the Grill Room showed the less formal face of The Savoy, a kind of stars' canteen for the actors at the Savoy Theatre across the courtyard. It attracted a more intimate café society, led by Noel Coward and Gertrude Lawrence, who at one time were permanent fixtures.

The Grill Room had, and has, its own *maître-chef*, a post then held by Jean-Baptiste Virlogeux, a huge, gouty man who was never actually seen to cook anything, but who tasted everything with intensity. In order to provide himself with the imposing sculpted figure that befitted his position, he would encase himself in a vast corset and periodically embark on a spartan *régime* of boiled cabbage, an apple and a glass of milk. After a few week's dieting had made no appreciable difference he would crack and revert to his former gargantuan meals.

By 1930, the exterior of The Savoy had changed

radically, as if anticipating the look of the Thirties. It was then that the extraordinary stainless steel canopy in Savoy Court, designed by architects Easton and Robertson and today the most familar vista of the hotel, first made its dramatic appearance. Underneath was the Savoy Theatre: the old one was demolished in June 1929, to be replaced just 135 days later by a new air-conditioned auditorium with a built-in automatic vacuum cleaner like the hotel. It had been designed by Frank Tugwell and decorated by Basil Ionides, using

ONE OF THE LEGENDARY BATHROOMS WITH ITS ORIGINAL FITTINGS BY BASIL IONIDES

five thousand books of silver leaf and two thousand superficial feet of ebony.

But behind all this flamboyance and big spending lay the grim reality of the Depression and the threat of a new war in Europe. The Savoy made a loss for the first time in its history, and it took the early precaution of closing the glass-domed restaurant and moving diners to the relative safety of the basement. Carroll Gibbons, who had been on holiday in America when war broke out, won the hearts of Savoy patrons when he battled through red tape and got back to England to resume his leadership of the Savoy Orpheans, and played through the war.

During and after the war food rationing brought special problems for the Restaurant staff. Although certain commodities remained reasonably plentiful others were in short supply. The professional challenge, for a chef like François Latry who was accustomed to cooking with the best ingredients in the world, lay in finding ways to make appetising and sustaining food out of limited resources. He rose magnificiently to the occasion and devised what was to become his most famous dish. It was to Latry's great credit that the Woolton Pie, named after the Minister for Food and containing potatoes, parsnips, leeks and carrots, became a staple item in most homes.

and a single liqueur and – eh voilà! Until, that is, a Cabinet Minister frowned the practice out of existence.

As for drink, judicious pre-war purchasing had ensured that wines, brandies and liqueurs, although rationed, were not in short supply: at no time was there any serious risk of the cellars running dry. At this time the head cellarman was the extraordinary J. M. Eggle, like Hitler a native of Linz, who seldom stopped work before midnight. He was famous for his mistrust of waiters, saying, 'There is only one difference between a waiter and the devil – a waiter has two tails'.

In the war the American Bar became the unofficial HQ of the U.S. war correspondents, perhaps because

THE SAVOY

has London's most complete Shelter. At night the Restaurant is transferred to the Shelter.

Carroll Gibbons and the Savoy Hotel Orpheans play for dancing, and Vic Oliver appears at midnight.

Arthur Salisbury and his Orchestra play during Dinner.

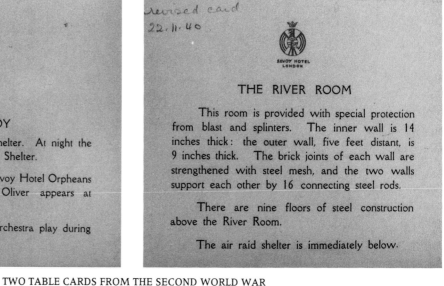

revised card
22.11.40.

THE RIVER ROOM

This room is provided with special protection from blast and splinters. The inner wall is 14 inches thick: the outer wall, five feet distant, is 9 inches thick. The brick joints of each wall are strengthened with steel mesh, and the two walls support each other by 16 connecting steel rods.

There are nine floors of steel construction above the River Room.

The air raid shelter is immediately below.

TWO TABLE CARDS FROM THE SECOND WORLD WAR
REVEALING THE HOTEL'S IMPERTURBABILITY

The usual quota permitted for restaurants was an ounce of meat per diner, and the total bill was not to exceed five shillings. (Before the war a sirloin steak had been four shillings and sixpence and a bottle of vintage Bollinger thirty-five shillings.) Bread was not to be offered unless a diner specifically requested it, a regulation which led to an awkward incident when it was unthinkingly given to some men from the Ministry. But as a designated First Class Establishment the hotel was allowed a little leeway in catering matters. Though *Crêpes Suzette* was a prohibited dish, it was possible for a diner to order a pancake, a single brandy

women were not yet permitted in the bar (a state of affairs not rectified until 1947). The legendary Harry Craddock had retired by then and the journalists called the new barman Vic – well, they *called* him Vic, but his name was actually Johnny Johnson. He was succeeded by Joe Gilmore, who was also known as Vic by the habitués.

Latry retired in 1942, giving way to another Frenchman, Marious Sylvan Dutrey, who achieved the notable feat of securing a reasonable supply of venison and smoked herring from a Scottish contact of Hugh Wontner, Managing Director of The Savoy

Group. Even so, it is said that at one stage Dutrey was seriously contemplating the best way of preparing owl. The following year Camille Payard took over but, sadly, he died of a heart attack in 1946, to be replaced by Auguste Laplanche, a Norman who served The Savoy as *maître-chef* for nearly twenty years.

Working with simple ingredients was less stressful to Laplanche than it had been to Latry, whose instinctive preference was for a more florid style of cookery, but even so, when rationing was finally over, Laplanche used more than a ton of Normandy butter every week, and dishes from Normandy such as *Tripes à la Mode de Caen* and *Canard à la Rouennaise* began to appear on The Savoy's menu. Laplanche's cooking had one particularly distinguished fan – Sir Winston Churchill, who once dined at The Savoy five times in a fortnight. Shortly after the war he also had the honour of cooking for King George VI at the hotel, the first reigning monarch to visit it.

The music played on; Lena Horne sang at The Savoy in the fifties, Josephine Baker in the sixties; and in those Swinging Sixties the hotel became the reluctant centre of press attention when it attempted to hold out against the invasion of the trouser suits. Cathy McGowan, the presenter of ITV's pop programme 'Ready Steady Go!', hit the headlines in 1965 when she was politely turned away from the Restaurant for wearing a trouser suit in the evening. 'We do rather deplore gimmicky clothes,' said a Savoy director, 'particularly with a photographer in the background with the intention of getting a headline.' That was a gauntlet thrown down to Fleet Street, and for five years any self-respecting starlet needing tabloid coverage first attempted to breach the Savoy defences in a trouser suit. Twiggy managed it in 1966 (in orange cords) but it was claimed that the manager had mistaken her for a boy. Lady Whitmore maintained she was the first to be accepted in one, but then attention shifted to men's polo neck shirts, of which Lord Snowdon was a leading exponent. In 1968 the actor David Hemmings was refused admission to the Restaurant because he was wearing a brown corduroy jacket. By 1971 The Savoy's sartorial resistance had crumbled; hot pants were seen in the Grill, although it was still deemed worthy of a press mention.

Within fifteen years guests at a Savoy wedding reception were to gasp at the sight of a stunning pink trouser suit, an exquisite hairstyle, flawless make-up, a jewelled choker at the throat – and that was just the bridegroom. Nick Rhodes, the Duran Duran keyboard player, was getting married in a fantasy of pink. Among the guests were several live flamingos. The tradition of the great Savoy parties lives on: in 1984 Aldo Gucci, whose grandfather had a somewhat different relationship to the hotel, had one of the great rooms converted into a Tuscan grove for his guests,

SIR WINSTON CHURCHILL ACKNOWLEDGING THE CROWDS AS HE ARRIVES AT THE HOTEL FOR A DINNER OF THE OTHER CLUB

who included the Prince and Princess of Wales, Edward Heath and Luciano Pavarotti.

Over the years some rare and wonderful culinary experiments have been carried out in response to guests' wishes. At the Woman of the Year Luncheon in 1964, The Savoy produced a 1,900-year-old recipe for sole with lovage, which they called *Patina Solearum*

Farius Apicius. The hardest task Laplanche had was tracking down the lovage, which he eventually found in a Kentish farm. As Madame Ritz claimed to be the inspiration of Escoffier's *Toast Melba*, so Paolo Contarini, the then general manager, claimed the credit for Laplanche's most astonishing dessert, *Mousse Glacée Cléopatra*. It is a highly elaborate concoction, created for the opening night party of the epic film *Cleopatra* starring Elizabeth Taylor in 1963, and is a dish only a grand hotel could dream of serving:

'For fifteen people, take twelve eggs, separate them and place the yolks with a gill of syrup in a bain-marie *at 320°F. Cook them gently till they thicken, then beat till cold and light. Beat the egg whites till stiff, then add sugar and water heated to 240°F and beat again until cold. Add the meringue mixture to the yolk mixture, then beat in a quart of double cream and a quarter bottle of Green Chartreuse until the whole is light and fluffy. Add several ounces of Rosolio liqueur bonbons, pour the mousse into a specially made pyramidal mould, and place in a refrigerator to set. Serve on a silver dish garnished with sliced peaches, strawberries, raspberries and pineapple covered in Grand Marnier sauce, made from two pounds of apricot sauce, the juice of ten oranges, half a pound of raspberry purée and Grand Marnier liqueur. Top the pyramid with Sauce Chartreuse, made from a pound of apricot sauce, the juice of six oranges and Green Chartreuse.'*

On Laplanche's retirement in 1965 Silvino Trompetto, who had been the Grill chef since 1962, took over as the first non-French *maître-chef* at The Savoy. Despite his name, Trompetto had been born in Westminster, of Italian parents. His *Quenelles de Brochet Sauce Bercy* has already reached classic status in international cuisine, likewise his lobster mousse. He canned truffles himself in Madeira wine. Although Savoy cooking has always been predominantly French, English dishes are also available on the menu; Trompetto's Steak and Kidney Pie was a particular favourite, as was his Bread and Butter Pudding. By 1983 the tradition of long service had been re-established, with only two *maître-chefs* since the war. Having achieved the accolade of being the first chef to

THE SAVOY PORTER AWAITS THE ARRIVAL OF
AMERICAN GUESTS AT SOUTHAMPTON DOCKS

receive the MBE, it was time for Trompetto to hand over the ladle to a younger man.

In its hundred year history, the control of The Savoy Group, including Claridge's, The Connaught, The Berkeley, as well as The Savoy itself, has been in the hands of remarkably few men. D'Oyly Carte on his retirement entrusted the Group to George Reeves-Smith. As his own career drew to a close, Reeves-Smith was impressed by the professionalism of a young man named Hugh Wontner. Wontner joined The Savoy in 1938 and when Reeves-Smith retired in 1942, he took over as Managing Director. He successfully took the Group through the war years and was subsequently knighted and became Lord Mayor of London.

When Wontner came to contemplate his own retirement, Giles Shepard was appointed Managing Director of the Group. Like Sir George Reeves-Smith, Shepard had a background in the drinks business. After Eton and the Coldstream Guards, he worked for a brewery and a cider company. It was while he was a director of another hotel, the Dorchester, that Sir Hugh Wontner approached him to talk about the succession. Shepard was flattered and enthusiastic, but his business eye saw that the structure of the Group, while outwardly sound, was not as solid as it could have been.

Bluntly, the hotel was losing money. The standard of service was, as always, impeccable, but in the years that it did not make a loss, the small profits were not a satisfactory return on capital invested. This made the Group vulnerable to predators and Shepard's task was three-fold and immediate: he had to maintain standards, raise profits and fight off unwelcome take-overs. With supreme adroitness he achieved all these aims. The Savoy Group which posted a £1.6 million loss in 1980, made a profit of £12.1 million in 1986. His staff are aware that they work in the world's most famous hotel and they have each acquired a cachet in their varied roles. Under the directorship of Giles Shepard they now have a secure framework in which to perfect their craft.

Behind this great hotel there is also a great woman. Olive Barnett came to work at The Savoy in 1928, and she still visits today to check that the astonishingly high standards she set for her staff are being carried forward. Miss Barnett, who worked for Sir George and then Sir Hugh as personal assistant, was instrumental in setting up The Savoy's world-famous Professional and Technical Training Department, became the doyenne of the British hotel business, and was awarded the OBE in 1981. She is regarded with affection springing from awe by the world's finest hoteliers. Giles Shepard went on an overseas trip with her shortly after he had been appointed Managing Director in 1979. He was shown to his pleasant but unexceptional room in a grand hotel, then went to

JUDY GARLAND'S CABARET APPEARANCES IN THE FIFTIES ARE STILL REMEMBERED BY GUESTS

collect Miss Barnett for dinner. Her vast, sumptuous suite cascaded with flowers and fruit, her verandah overlooked the most magnificent view, and Shepard realised that as mere Managing Director of The Savoy Group, he would always take second place in the eyes of the hotel manager to the formidable woman who had taught him his trade.

Under Giles Shepard, whose role as The Savoy Group's Managing Director involves responsibility for the group's overall financial interests, there are two figures who are today's equivalent of Ritz and Escoffier. They are the hotel's Managing Director and General Manager Willy Bauer and its *maître-chef* Anton Edelmann, the team who strive tirelessly to maintain the high standards which the Savoy's guests expect. Like many people in the hotel business, both men come from southern Germany, and both are of the opinion that no one has perfected the art of enjoyment like the British upper classes.

Willy Bauer has worked in Britain for twenty-five years. His job, in a nutshell, is to ensure that The Savoy remains the best hotel in the world. The way he achieves this is best summed up by his attitude to his place of work. He used to be assistant manager of a hotel in Swansea. 'It was the best hotel in Wales,' he said. 'I believed it. I felt it. If I thought it was the best, then it had to be the best. Everything I do has to be for the best; it's a policy of perfection – nothing else will do. What is the point in doing something if you don't intend it to be the best you can do?' He works long hours, constantly looking after the needs of the hotel and guests. Three times a day he is seen in the front hall meeting people, and the staff say of him 'he is on stage three times a day and in the wings the rest of it'.

It was Sir Hugh Wontner who gave Bauer the most demanding job briefing imaginable when he was appointed Managing Director – demanding, but short: 'Never compromise.' He accepted the brief with enthusiasm. 'A hotel manager is not just a businessman,' he says. 'He is a specialist in food, wine, interior design, housekeeping, public relations, technical service etc – it's a never ending challenge with unlimited potential. Hotel life is exciting! I deal with royalty and the kitchen porter and I enjoy having to deal with problems and make them right.' A youthful fifty, Bauer admires the example of Sir Hugh Wontner, who retired in 1984 but who still comes in to work at the hotel five days a week. But then retirement is inconceivable to both Bauer and Edelmann, today's Savoy team: you might as well ask a bee when it would stop making honey.

From the start The Savoy has been an international hotel; it was inspired in its concept, amenities and service by the pioneer American luxury hotels; in its food by France and the rest of Europe; in its enter-tainment by the best in the world; in its demeanour by the lazy, friendly elegance of the British aristocrat. This spirit of internationalism is one that is proudly maintained by Bauer and his staff today. They are at ease with all nationalities and intend, with the utmost charm, tact and diplomacy, to keep the mix as it is – so the guest in the resplendent costume at the table next to yours could be from Mongolia, Mozambique or Mexico.

Given a certain level of prosperity, the best eating is to be had not by an endless quest for the new and bizarre but in finding the best source of the classic ingredients. In this The Savoy has an unquestioned advantage. A top-class restaurant may do a hundred *couverts* in an evening: The Savoy Restaurant has to equal or better the standard with up to three hundred *couverts*. How many restaurants can boast eighty chefs? Because of this unique combination of quantity and quality The Savoy, untrammelled by accountants bleating about portion control and price purchasing, can and does buy the best meat in the world.

The old xenophobic defence of British cookery was that the basic materials were so fine that they needed little in the way of enhancement, whereas the French had to disguise the inferior quality of their meats with a bewildering diversity of sauces. The fact that The Savoy insists on Scotch beef, English pork and Welsh lamb shows that the legend is half-true. The meal you enjoy at The Savoy will be made from the finest ingredients, and prepared with all the skill and care that has made it renowned for so long.

The main restaurant is stylish and extremely comfortable, with a bandstand and a dance floor in proper Savoy tradition. The bandstand was designed by Carl Toms and Lord Snowdon in 1983, a remarkable construction of chandelier glass and a Portuguese slate floor, with gunmetal and brass columns.

The Grill Room, formerly known as the Café Parisien, still has its own *maître-chef* and kitchens, and the food is, as one might expect, not a whit less fine; the Grill simply provides an alternative to the classic *haute cuisine* of the Restaurant.

Recently even further choice has been provided by the inclusion of a brasserie, 'Upstairs at The Savoy', the brainchild of Willy Bauer. 'Upstairs' – an intriguing name: 'Let me take you to lunch Upstairs at The Savoy!' – is a delicious surprise. On the first floor there used to be a small and very exclusive shopping arcade with tiny boutiques. Bauer's brainwave was to convert this arcade into a brasserie, and to commission David Mlinaric to design the cool and sophisticated room, with a Cruvinet machine so that individual glasses of fine wine can be served without the necessity of the bottle being finished at one expensive sitting: it will keep the opened wine in perfect condition for months. Overlooking the hotel's main entrance

A banquet at The Savoy promises to be something special, and it is. The food comes from the Restaurant kitchen, therefore it is under the direction of Anton Edelmann himself. One of the groups that regularly holds banquets at The Savoy is called the Savoy Gastronomes; as its members include managers of luxury hotels all over the world, it would not do to serve anything less than the very best.

Original music scores line the walls of the corridor leading to the Private Rooms, each one of which is named after a Gilbert and Sullivan opera. In 1943, in

CHARLIE CHAPLIN AND HIS WIFE WERE FREQUENT VISITORS IN POST-WAR YEARS

CLEANING SILVER – A DAILY RITUAL AT THE SAVOY

and the Savoy Theatre, one can observe unobserved.

Then there is the banqueting level, which has its own entrance on the Embankment with a distinctive *porte cochère*. The banqueting suites range from luxurious little rooms for an intimate *dîner à deux* to the opulence of the enormous Lancaster Room, formerly known as the Ballroom (the original courtyard of the hotel when the main entrance was in Savoy Hill). Five hundred can dine there in comfort.

the room called 'Patience', Benelux was created by the Foreign Ministers of Belgium, the Netherlands and Luxembourg: the first successful attempt to provide a customs-free trading area in Europe.

The Other Club, founded in 1911 by Winston Churchill and Lord Birkenhead, consists of thirty members, half politicians, half scholars and lawyers. Once a month they still dine at The Savoy, usually in the Pinafore Room, where Kaspar sits on a shelf.

HOW THE GLORIOUS TWELFTH WAS CELEBRATED IN 1987

Kaspar is a black wooden cat carved in 1926 by Basil Ionides, who designed the decor for the Savoy Theatre. If there is a party of thirteen, Kaspar has a place set to make up the numbers to fourteen. He disappeared during the war just after a party of RAF officers had dined rather well in the room. When Winston Churchill dined with The Other Club a fortnight later, he noticed its loss. Within a week Kaspar was back, some say all the way from Singapore.

Somehow one remembers chefs of the *ancien régime* as slow, massive and stately; god-like beings inhabiting a boned and rolled world outside the normal dimensions of life. The new chefs are very different. Anton Edelmann is the very model of the modern *maître-chef*

de cuisine, bristling with energy, alert as a hare. Unlike his illustrious predecessors he has no difficulty with the English language, and in a torrent of words pours out his enthusiasm for cooking, for The Savoy, for life.

Edelmann came to England from Munich in 1971 and started at The Savoy under Silvino Trompetto. From the very first day he knew he wanted to be *maître-chef de cuisine* at the most famous hotel in the world, so when he left to pursue his career elsewhere, it was in the certain knowledge that one day he would be back at The Savoy. He has been there for six years now, and he is still dumbfounded by it. 'Nobody would build a hotel like this nowadays. They'd have to be mad to do such a thing, it is not logical, genius is not logical. That's why it's so nice to be a guest here; it is a voyage of perpetual discovery.'

When Edelmann took over, the first project he set

in hand was the total redesign and rebuilding of the kitchens. A temporary kitchen had to be built at a cost of £500,000, while Escoffier's old ovens, which had been in continuous use from 1895 to 1985, were finally mothballed. The new kitchen, on the first floor in order to be right next to the Restaurant, has cost £3.5 million and is not yet, at the time of writing, quite complete, though H.M. Queen Elizabeth, the Queen Mother, visited it on 5th December 1985.

With the air-conditioning on full blast, the temperature in the kitchen, summer or winter, is a steady 80°F (25°C). 'Never have a cold kitchen. Temperature is of the utmost importance. A cold room – even a cold draught – kills the taste. I say the refrigerator is the bane of food taste. Even cold meats should be warmer – just slightly under room temperature, say. Heat brings out the flavour. That's why we cook food.'

Edelmann is in charge of a carefully structured team. There are the *sous-chefs* who keep an eye on day-to-day operations, the *chefs-de-partie* with their own special area of responsibility – Meat and Game, Fish and so on – and they in turn have their own staff of five or six *commis chefs*. He is, however, acutely aware that he is ultimately responsible for every morsel of food that is prepared in the Restaurant kitchen, and he is forever tasting, sampling, smelling, checking.

As a luxury hotel The Savoy has to be able to provide the best of everything. But the best food, Edelmann insists, is not necessarily the rarest or the most expensive. Talking of food spurs this normally animated and enthusiastic man to near messianic heights. There are highly prized foods; there are foods which are difficult or impossible to grow or rear – the truffle, Colette's 'black pearl of gastronomy', has never been successfully cultivated commercially, and because of its rarity must always remain expensive. Some may consider that the truffle is overrated; Edelmann would not agree. 'It is impossible, it is worth all that is said for it, and more!' He dismisses the normal encounter most people have with them – a sliver of tasteless black rubber on top of a pâté – and describes how to treat a truffle properly for the best reward. 'You take the truffle, fresh of course, and you macerate it in vintage port for a few days. The resulting juice is delicious beyond belief, and is used to make sauce of astonishing pungency.'

Supply and demand has its effect on taste, as does food snobbery. Twenty years ago the kiwi fruit was almost unknown in this country; now it is on a par with Black Forest gâteau in the estimation of many gourmets. Edelmann is a supporter of the maligned fruit – a good one, simply peeled and eaten whole, is not only delicious but has one of the highest vitamin C yields of any fruit. The best food, repeats Edelmann, is the freshest. The Savoy uses only fresh food. If you must eat strawberries and raspberries in January, they will be available and they will be fresh, but please do

ANTON EDELMANN

not ask the price. As George Reeves-Smith once said, The Savoy is expensive, but never dear.

Edelmann admits to appreciating his food more when he is under less pressure. Dealing daily with every known luxury foodstuff, it is difficult to imagine what sort of food he could possibly choose as a treat. To many of us a feast would consist of the aristocratic rarities we can seldom afford – caviar, smoked salmon, foie gras, champagne, oysters, fillet steak, lobster – whereas The Savoy sees these daily. So what delicacies can tempt his palate?

THAT'S ENTERTAINMENT IN THE HOTEL BALLROOM:
CYD CHARISSE, GENE KELLY AND FRED ASTAIRE

Novelty is out for a start. As Edelmann points out, anything worth eating has already been discovered. The reason why snail's egg caviar was not a major delicacy until a couple of years ago is simply that it is not that wonderful a taste experience. It is not offered at The Savoy, though if you could not live without it, it would no doubt be procured for you.

True excellence is to be found in the simplest things. Not so long ago Edelmann had a piece of beef, plainly cooked. It was, he says, outstandingly, indescribably glorious: the texture and flavour were, were – he searches for the right words and fails – 'like meaty butter'. Traced to its source, it was a pure bred Angus from the Hebrides, one of only fourteen left. So many Aberdeen Angus are now crossed with Charolais that the true flavour has been extenuated and we forget how superlative it is, until something like that plain piece of beef comes along to jolt our tastebuds out of their complacency.

Complaining that he has little time to eat, Edelmann polishes off a three-course lunch with evident pleasure: quickly, enthusiastically and completely, yet he remains energetically trim. With a minimum of a fourteen-hour working day he has no time to slump in front of a television set for relaxation *à la mode anglaise*, for when he is not at work he sleeps. The thought of this sort of do-nothing lull is unappealing to him; it would mean a double life.

There is an interesting comparison to be drawn between the daily life of two men, Escoffier and Edelmann, doing the same job but separated by a hundred years. Here, in his own words, is Anton Edelmann's day:

6.30 Rise, and the essential cup of tea to start the motor running.

7.00 Drive to The Savoy. Strictly no car phone, but a tape recorder keeps thoughts marshalled, and dictation is done ready for typing. Most of the recipes in this book started this way.

8.00 Another cup of tea, and the morning kitchen inspection. The toque is always worn.

8.45 Meeting with the *chefs de partie* – there are fourteen, each responsible for a group of cooks who specialise in sauces, pâtisserie, entrées, etc. There are now some female chefs at The Savoy – ten years ago Trompetto would rarely allow a woman into his kitchens.

9.00 Checking the day's orders have been correctly fulfilled; administration.

9.45 Savoy Heads of Departments' meeting with Willy Bauer,

the Managing Director and General Manager of the hotel.

10.00 Control and supervise cooking for lunch.

2.00 Prepare the orders for tomorrow's food.

3.00 A quick lunch with three or four of the six *sous-chefs*.

3.30 General administration, menu writing, proof-reading.

5.30 The right stuff. Some actual cooking is done now, although with eighty chefs at work in the kitchens it is sometimes difficult to find a niche.

9.30 Shower and change, leave the hotel.

10.30 Home.

For holidays Edelmann travels – to eat at other restaurants. He went into cooking simply because he loved food, and one regret of his early life was that while training as a cook, there was neither the money nor the leisure to sample other people's cookery. So every year he goes on a busman's holiday around

TELEVISION PERSONALITY MICHAEL PARKINSON IS PRESENTED WITH A SURPRISE BIRTHDAY CAKE MADE BY HIS SON NICHOLAS, AT THAT TIME A YOUNG COMMIS CHEF IN THE GRILL KITCHEN

Europe, putting on two of three kilos of research. Vigorous games of squash and the heat of The Savoy kitchens take it off again soon enough.

Although both Edelmann and Bauer have strong personalities, rather than superimpose them on the character of the hotel, they both feel that they are upholding the tradition of excellence that has characterised The Savoy from the days of D'Oyly Carte and Ritz. Along with the rest of the staff, they also share an unashamed admiration for the skills of everyone else

THE EARLY MORNING ROUND OF THE MEAT BUYER AT SMITHFIELD MARKET

CHAMPAGNE, CHABLIS AND SEAFOOD
UPSTAIRS AT THE SAVOY

on the team. Francis 'Eddie' Edwards, the chief carver at the hotel, recently made an instructional video on carving techniques, and a small party was held to launch it. Later Bauer described the event correctly and formally – Eddie had carved a duck by way of demonstration – but after he had finished his analytical dissection of Eddie's technique, he shook his head slightly and quietly added: 'It was perfection.' His respect was profound. In the hands of Willy Bauer and Anton Edelmann, the quest for excellence continues into the hotel's second century.

A Savoy Day

MORNING WATCH 4–8

The early morning is quiet, but never still. As always, the hotel is full. Some guests are talking to colleagues in Australia and Japan. Others are still celebrating from the night before. Most are sleeping peacefully in their exceptionally comfortable beds, in somnolent ignorance of the fact that their good night's sleep is perhaps due to superb horsehair mattresses manufactured by The Savoy itself in its small factory in Covent Garden. People have been so impressed by the Savoy mattresses that they insisted on buying one (or two), undeterred by the price of £1,000. Down in the front hall a lady serenely polishes the brass full time, five days a week.

As day breaks, the guests stir luxuriously awake. The hotel never sleeps. Down in the kitchen breakfast is being prepared – the best croissants this side of Paris are being baked, the mighty British breakfast is being constructed. Up in the suites the baths fill silently; alas, this is gradually being phased out as distracted guests sometimes forget the water is running and the bath overflows. But no-one can forget the showerheads – ah, the showerheads! A full foot in diameter, the jets come out like rods. It is a massage and a shower at the same time. Whirlpool baths pale into insignificance by comparison.

FORENOON WATCH 8–12

Guests are up and about their business; the day staff have taken over. Underneath the main part of the hotel the service departments are humming with activity. There are two table men, whose sole function is moving tables. Behind the banqueting rooms, even now busy as tables are moved and cleaners polish in preparation for the lunchtime functions, lies the original entrance to the hotel in Savoy Hill, now only used by royalty, who need inconspicuous access.

One of the least known streets in London is Savoy Way, a public thoroughfare running through the middle of the hotel. The hotel is above, below and on either side of the road. The Flower Department, the Meat Department and the cold store give on to the road, which is usually impassable, being jammed with delivery lorries. Many of the world's leading hoteliers owe their style and knowledge to The Savoy's renow-

WINNER OF A NATIONAL NEWSPAPER BINGO COMPETITION ENJOYING A CHAMPAGNE BREAKFAST

ned five-year management training scheme which starts off with a month in the Meat Department.

AFTERNOON WATCH 12–4

A guest who thinks she is too busy for lunch needs to fax an urgent message to her San Francisco office. Today she has to go down to the ground floor to The Savoy telecommunications bureau off the Thames Foyer which supplies the telephone, telex and telefax service to guests, but by the Centenary 16-channel cable television will be in all the guests' rooms, as well as the facility to interface with their own personal computers world-wide.

Just as guests' preferences used to be kept on orange cards, they are now computerised. The wood panelled Communications Room, like a ship's bridge, has six brass clocks on the wall, showing the time in Paris, Frankfurt, New York, San Francisco, Tokyo and Sydney. On the way back to her room the busy guest passes the Grill, and decides that perhaps she is not that busy after all.

DOG WATCHES   4–8

The ornate mirrors on the walls of the Thames Foyer, once the centre of the main restaurant, were redis-

SIGNED PHOTOGRAPHS COVER A WALL OF THE
PRESS OFFICE

covered while the room was being redecorated with the *trompe l'oeil* mural, painted by Lincoln Taber in 1980. He painted a crumpled tea towel on one wall so realistically that waiters used to try to pick it up. He also added a fly, but so many people tried to swat it that the whole surrounding area became dirty and it had to be painted out.

Preparations begin for the evening's festivities. There is always something being celebrated at The Savoy. Valets on each floor await the guests' calls.

They are always on hand to steam out the creases, or iron them back in. If as a guest you are lucky enough to catch a valet in a quiet moment, ask for a tale or two, but please do not laugh too loudly as you may disturb the other guests. You will hear tales of evening dresses falling into baths twenty minutes before the ball, of distraught dowagers locked in their bathrooms (there are bells to summon help in every room). In each case the guest has been restored to something approaching equilibrium. Very few people are now accustomed to receiving such service at home but The Savoy has a staff-to-guest ratio of three-to-one. The evening dress disaster is not uncommon – it is a well-known traveller's trick to get the creases out of clothes by hanging them in a steamy bathroom – but at The Savoy there is no need because the valets are quicker and better at pressing clothes than anyone else in the world – even a Fortuny gown would pose no problem.

FIRST WATCH   8–12

In the gentlemen's cloakroom a spiral iron staircase leads to the upper room where the top hats were kept. Shortly after the last war a recently ennobled Labour peer, astonished that he never had to produce his ticket before his topper was instantly handed to him, found the reason in a slip inside which read, 'Ugly bugger. Big nose.' There are 120 diners in the Restaurant and 85 *couverts* in the Grill Room. In the River Room a party to relaunch a motoring publisher is being given. The first night of a major new film is to be celebrated in the Lancaster Room. One of the diners in Iolanthe, a private room, looks as if he could be the German Head of State. He is. A flushed young man angrily sends back his second bottle of wine because 'it's corked'. The perfect wine is replaced without demur. Boisterous laughter comes from a table in the Grill Room. An elderly woman eating alone in her room on the fifth floor turns out her light to look out over the Thames in the moonlight and see what Monet saw. Downstairs in the kitchen 800 meals of an uncompromisingly high quality have been served. The flushed young man is in love.

MIDDLE WATCH   12–4

At any time of the day or night someone somewhere in The Savoy will be washing a dish. Now there are mighty industrial machines to do most of the work, but with seven different designs of china and up to twelve thousand separate pieces in each collection to look after, the task is too complex for mere machines. The services are simply called Courtside, Hotelside, Upstairs, Restaurant, Grill, Private Rooms and Banqueting Rooms. Being a dishwasher at The Savoy has some fine precedents – at the turn of the century an immigrant dishwasher called Guccio Gucci was so astounded by the glamour and wealth of the guests that he went home to Florence to manufacture luxury leather goods for them.　　　　GWYN HEADLEY

ALDO GUCCI, THE PRINCE AND PRINCESS OF WALES AND
WILLY BAUER

LES
HORS-D'ŒUVRE

OMELETTE OTHELLO

OTHELLO OMELET

Chaliapin – nicknamed ''Charlie Pine'' by Lady Diana Cooper – always had a suite at the Savoy when he was singing at the Royal Opera House in Covent Garden. His charismatic personality endeared him to all the staff, particularly the chef Latry who appropriately christened this omelet Othello. Chaliapin was one of the few guests who dared to walk into the chef's office without warning to share anecdotes and taste new dishes.

Mix together the mayonnaise, tomato catsup, horseradish, yogurt and orange juice. Add the chives and

1 cup less 2 Tbsp/200 ml mayonnaise (page 199)
½ cup less 1 Tbsp/100 ml tomato catsup
2 tsp/10 g freshly grated horseradish
½ cup less 1 Tbsp/100 ml natural yogurt
¼ cup/50 ml orange juice
4 Tbsp/10 g freshly snipped chives
Tabasco sauce
1 cup/125 g white crab meat
2 oz/50 g smoked salmon, cut in *julienne*
2½ Tbsp/40 g diced plum tomato fillets
8 eggs
4 Tbsp/10 g freshly chopped herbs
2½ Tbsp/40 g unsalted butter
assorted salad leaves
¼ cup/50 ml salad dressing (page 201)
salt and freshly milled pepper

Serves 4

season with salt, pepper and a dash of Tabasco sauce.

Mix the crab meat with the smoked salmon and tomato, and add a spoonful of the prepared sauce.

Beat the eggs and herbs with salt and pepper and use to make eight small flat egg crêpes, using a little of the butter for each one. Divide the filling between the egg crêpes and fold each in half.

Mix the salad leaves with the salad dressing, season with salt and pepper and arrange some at the top of each plate. Place two filled crêpes in the center of each plate and pour some sauce over the crêpes.

GOURMET DELIGHT

**SHOWN IN ENGLISH
ON SAVOY MENUS**

Chop the fillet of beef very finely. Add the egg yolks, onion, capers, gherkins, parsley and anchovies, and mix well. Season to taste with paprika, Tabasco sauce, Worcestershire sauce, brandy, salt and pepper.

Stamp out eight 2-inch/5-cm circles of bread and fry in half the butter.

1¼ lb/550 g fillet of beef, trimmed
2 egg yolks
2½ Tbsp/15 g minced onion
1⅔ Tbsp/10 g minced capers
1 Tbsp/10 g minced gherkins
4 Tbsp/10 g finely chopped parsley
2½ medium anchovy fillets, finely chopped
paprika
Tabasco sauce
Worcestershire sauce
brandy
4 slices of bread
2⅔ Tbsp/40 g unsalted butter
1⅓ Tbsp/20 g Beluga caviar
4 quails' eggs
salt and freshly milled pepper
fresh chive tops
salad greens

Serves 4

Divide the beef mixture into eight equal portions and mold each to fit a *croûte*. Garnish four of the beef *croûtes* with the caviar. Melt the remaining butter and fry the quails' eggs. Use to garnish the remaining beef *croûtes*.

Garnish with fresh chives and salad greens.

TERRINE
D'HOMARD ROMILLY

LOBSTER TERRINE ROMILLY

Remove the lobster eggs from under the tail fins. Cook the lobsters, one at a time, in the boiling vegetable stock for 5 minutes. Drain and refresh, reserving the vegetable stock. Carefully remove the shells from the lobster without damaging the tails. Reserve the four lobster claws.

Reserve ½ cup/100 g of the fish mousse. Pass the lobster eggs through a very fine strainer and add to the remaining fish mousse. Add three-quarters of the diced vegetables and the diced truffle, and mix thoroughly.

Bring the heavy cream to a boil. add a pinch of saffron strands and simmer until the cream becomes a very dark yellow. Leave to cool, then add the reserved fish mousse and the remaining diced vegetables. Mix well.

Separate the outside layers of the leeks and trim the green parts neatly. Blanch in boiling salted water until tender. Refresh, dry on a dish towel and season with salt and pepper.

Line a 5½-cup/1.5-liter terrine with plastic wrap, then line the bottom and sides with the leek, allowing some of it to hang over the edges.

Dry the spinach leaves on a dish cloth and lay out to the same length as the terrine and about 4-inches/10-cm

2 ×1 lb/450 g live hen lobsters with eggs, preferably Scottish
4 cups/1 liter vegetable stock (page 206)
3⅓ cups/675 g fish mousse (page 196)
⅓ cup/50 g finely diced carrot, blanched
½ cup/40 g finely diced leek, blanched
1⅓ Tbsp/10 g very finely diced truffle
½ cup less 1 Tbsp/100 ml heavy cream
saffron strands
2 whole leeks
¼ lb/100 g spinach leaves, blanched
½ cup/40 g tiny broccoli flowerets, blanched
8 cooked langoustine tails
1¾ cups/400 ml gazpacho coulis (page 196)
6 cooked lobster claws, shell removed
¼ cup/50 ml Savoy dressing (page 201)
salt and freshly milled pepper
dried lobster eggs (page 207), optional

Serves 10

wide. Season with salt and pepper. Spread the saffron mousse evenly over the spinach leaves. Place the lobster tails, overlapping the thin ends to one side of the mousse, and roll up to form a neat roulade.

Spoon a 1-inch/2.5-cm layer of lobster mousse into the prepared terrine, making a slight indentation along the center. Position the roulade of lobster in the center of the terrine and just cover with some of the remaining lobster mousse. Arrange the broccoli flowerets along the center of the terrine on top of the roulade and position the langoustine tails on either side. Cover with the remaining lobster mousse. Neatly fold the leek over the lobster mousse and cover with plastic wrap.

Poach in a water bath at 300°F/150°C for about 55 minutes until just firm. Leave the terrine to rest for about 30 minutes in a warm place.

Cut the terrine in slices and position one in the center of each plate. Spoon a little of the gazpacho coulis around each portion. Warm all the lobster claws in a little of the vegetable stock and toss in the Savoy dressing. Garnish each portion with a lobster claw and a few dried lobster eggs, if wished.

MARBRE DE FOIE DE CANARD ET LANGUE EN GELEE

DUCK LIVER AND VEAL TONGUE PATE IN ASPIC

2 Tbsp / 20 g raisins
½ cup less 1 Tbsp / 100 ml brandy
1½ lb / 675 g fresh duck liver
1 cup less 2 Tbsp / 200 ml ruby port
1 stick of cinnamon
⅔ cup / 150 ml Madeira sauce (page 198)
2 leaves of gelatin, soaked in a little water
1¼ Tbsp / 15 g sugar
2½ oz / 65 g veal tongue
1 onion piqué (page 181)
1¼ cups / 300 ml duck aspic (page 194)
salt and freshly milled pepper
10 tomato roses
20 fresh mint leaves

Serves 10

Cover the raisins with some of the brandy and leave to soak overnight. Drain and reserve any brandy.

Remove the skin and all the veins from the duck liver and cut in ½-inch/ 1-cm thick escalopes. Place these in a shallow dish and marinate overnight in the port and the remaining brandy with the stick of cinnamon.

Remove the liver escalopes and dry thoroughly. Reserve the marinade. Season the escalopes generously, then quickly seal in a very hot dry pan. Reduce the marinade and any reserved brandy from the raisins by two-thirds and add the Madeira sauce. Continue to reduce to a syrupy consistency. Add the soaked gelatin and the sugar to the warm reduction and season to taste.

Place the veal tongue in cold salted water and bring to a boil. Drain and refresh. Cook the blanched tongue in boiling salted water with the onion piqué until tender. Cool, remove the skin, and cut in ¾-inch/2-cm diameter batons.

Arrange one layer of marinated liver escalopes in a 3-cup/750-ml terrine. Brush a thin layer of the syrupy mixture on top and sprinkle with some of the raisins. Continue layering in this way until the terrine is half full. Position a line of veal tongue along the center of the terrine, then continue layering the escalopes and raisins until the terrine is full. Cover the terrine and weight down. Refrigerate overnight.

Unmold and cut the pâté in thin slices using a warmed knife. Position a slice on each plate. Finely chop the duck aspic and pipe a thin line around each slice of pâté. Garnish each slice with a tomato rose and two mint leaves. Serve with warm miniature brioches.

PATE DE CANARD SAUVAGE EN CROUTE FORESTIERE

WILD DUCK PATE IN A PASTRY CASE

3 wild ducks, dressed
⅔ cup/65 g mirepoix (page 207)
1 clove of garlic, chopped
24 peppercorns, crushed
1 bay leaf
1 cup less 2 Tbsp/200 ml brandy
2¼ cups/500 ml duck stock (page 194)
7 oz/200 g lean pork
9 oz/250 g pork fat
1 cup less 2 Tbsp/200 ml ruby port
finely grated peel of 1 orange
¼ cup/50 ml oil
2½ Tbsp/25 g chopped shallots
¼ cup/50 g unsalted butter
2 Tbsp/25 g skinned and roughly chopped pistachio nuts (page 207)
2 Tbsp/15 g chopped truffle
1½ lb/675 g dough for pâté en croûte (page 200)
9 oz/250 g salt pork, slightly frozen
5 oz/150 g goose liver pâté
1 egg yolk, beaten
4 cups/1 liter duck aspic with port (page 194)
1½ cups/100 g assorted wild mushrooms, cleaned
freshly chopped herbs
salt and freshly milled pepper
10 sprigs of mint
10 wild mushroom fleurons (page 206)
caramelized orange *julienne* (page 193)
1 cup/225 ml Cumberland sauce (page 195)

Serves 10

Remove the legs and breasts from the ducks. Remove the bones and all the skin from the legs. Chop all the bones and roast at 425°F/220°C for about 20 minutes. Add the mirepoix, garlic, peppercorns and bay leaf. Flame with half the brandy, add the duck stock and reduce by half, skimming frequently. Pass through a fine strainer.

Cut the meat from the duck legs, lean pork and pork fat in strips. Season with milled pepper, half the port and the orange peel and leave in the refrigerator for about 2 hours. Drain, reserving the marinade.

Finely grind the marinated meats twice, then pass through a fine strainer into a bowl set over ice. Mix well.

Season the duck breasts. Heat the oil and seal very quickly on both sides. Cool and marinate in the remaining brandy and port for at least 4 hours. Drain, reserving the marinade.

Sweat 2⅔ Tbsp/20 g of the shallots in 1 Tbsp/15 g of the butter, add both marinades and reduce. Add the duck stock and reduce to a glaze. Cool and thoroughly mix into the minced meats. Add the pistachio nuts and truffle, and season generously.

Roll out about three-quarters of the dough to about ⅛-inch/.3-cm thick and use to line a French-style 12 × 3 × 4½-inch /30 × 7.5 × 11.5-cm cast-iron terrine, allowing a little to overhang. Cut the salt pork in wafer-thin slices. Line the dough-lined terrine, allowing a little to overhang. Pack about one-third of the raw pâté

mixture into the terrine and position a line of goose liver pâté along the center. Cover with half the remaining raw pâté mixture and place the duck breasts along the center. Fill with the remaining raw pâté mixture and fold over the salt pork and dough. Brush the edges with egg yolk.

Roll out the remaining dough about ⅛-inch/.3-cm thick and trim to form a lid. Position on top and press the edges of the dough together to seal. Cut out a round opening to allow steam to escape and brush the surface of the dough with egg yolk. Garnish with the remaining dough trimmings and brush with egg yolk. Leave to rest for 20 minutes in the refrigerator.

Bake at 425°F/220°C for about 15 minutes, then reduce the heat to 350°F/180°C and bake for about 25 minutes. The pâté should be slightly pink inside. Leave to cool.

Melt the duck aspic, then leave until cool, but still liquid. Pour into the pâté en croûte through the opening to fill the space between the pâté and the pastry. Refrigerate overnight. Set the remaining aspic, then chop finely.

Sweat the remaining shallots in the remaining butter. Add the wild mushrooms and a sprinkling of fresh herbs. Season to taste.

Cut ½-inch/1-cm thick slices of the pâté. Position one slice on each plate. Garnish each portion with chopped aspic, a sprig of mint, a wild mushroom fleuron, wild mushrooms, orange *julienne* and Cumberland sauce.

PAUPIETTES DE SAUMON FUME FARCIES AU CRABE SAVOY

SMOKED SALMON PACKAGES

Mix the crab meat with the diced avocado, cucumber and tomato, and half the salad dressing. Season well with salt and pepper.

Divide the crab meat mixture between the slices of smoked salmon

1 cup/125 g flaked white crab meat
2 Tbsp/20 g diced avocado
2⅓ Tbsp/25 g seeded and diced cucumber
1⅓ Tbsp/20 g diced plum tomato fillets
5 Tbsp/75 ml salad dressing (page 201)
9 oz/250 g smoked salmon, cut in 8 thin slices
2⅔ Tbsp/40 g Beluga caviar
assorted salad leaves
salt and freshly milled pepper
chive tops

Serves 4

and fold each one into a neat package. Arrange two packages on each plate and top with the caviar. Toss the assorted salad leaves in the remaining salad dressing and season to taste. Arrange on plates and garnish with chive tops.

PETITE SALADE D'HOMARD ET D'ASPERGES

LOBSTER AND ASPARAGUS SALAD

2 × 1 lb/450 g live hen lobsters, preferably Scottish
4 cups/1 liter vegetable stock (page 206)
½ cup less 1 Tbsp/100 ml walnut oil
2 Tbsp/25 ml tarragon vinegar
superfine sugar
16 asparagus tips, cooked
assorted salad leaves
2 Tbsp/20 g thinly sliced fresh truffle
1⅓ Tbsp/20 g strips of plum tomato fillets
12 French green beans, blanched
salt and freshly milled pepper
8 sprigs of chervil

Serves 4

Cook the lobsters in the boiling vegetable stock for 10 minutes. Drain, reserving the stock, and refresh. Remove the shells. Cut both lobster tails into medallions.

Add the walnut oil to the vinegar and beat constantly until the mixture becomes almost white. Season with sugar, salt and pepper to taste.

Toss the asparagus tips in a little of the walnut dressing, season with salt and pepper and arrange on four plates.

Toss the assorted salad leaves in a little of the dressing and season. Arrange a small amount on each plate.

Gently warm the lobster medallions and claws in the reserved vegetable stock. Drain, then toss in some of the dressing and arrange the medallions and claws on the plates. Garnish with slices of truffle. Season the strips of tomato and green beans, toss in the dressing and arrange around the lobster. Garnish with sprigs of chervil.

PETITE SALADE
DE LANGOUSTINE JAPONAISE

LANGOUSTINE SALAD

16 cooked langoustine tails (pages 204 and 207)
⅔ cup/125 g green lentils, soaked in cold water for at least 4 hours
scant ¼ cup/40 g diced vegetables such as carrot, leek and celery
¼ cup/50 ml Savoy dressing (page 201)
1½-inch/4-cm piece of carrot
2¼-inch/6-cm piece of zucchini
1½ oz/40 g kohlrabi
1½ oz/40 g bacon
1 Tbsp/15 g unsalted butter
lollo rosso leaves
salad greens
chicory leaves
salt and freshly milled pepper
4 sprigs of fennel

Serves 4

Cut the langoustines in half and remove the intestines.

Cook the lentils in boiling salted water until well cooked. Drain and wash under cold running water. Cook the diced vegetables for 1 minute until *al dente*. Mix the green lentils and diced vegetables with a small amount of Savoy dressing. Season to taste.

Using a mandolin, cut the vegetables in "spaghetti." (Use only the green skin of the zucchini.)

Cut the bacon in ¼-inch/.5-cm wide strips and blanch in boiling water. Refresh and fry until very crisp in the butter.

Mix the langoustines with the vegetable "spaghetti" and bacon. Toss in a little of the Savoy dressing and season to taste with salt and pepper.

Place some of the green lentil mixture on each plate. Toss the salad leaves in a little of the Savoy dressing, arrange some on each plate and position the langoustine mixture on top. Garnish with sprigs of fennel.

PRALINE D'ŒUF DE CAILLE AU FOIE GRAS

QUAIL'S EGG WRAPPED IN FOIE GRAS

5 oz / 150 g Marbré de Canard (page 44)	
8 quails' eggs, soft-boiled and shelled (page 207)	
4 young spinach leaves, blanched	
2 hard-boiled egg white fillets, cut in 8 thin strips	
4 plum tomato diamonds	
1¼ cups / 300 ml duck aspic (page 194)	
12 orange segments (page 203)	
assorted salad leaves	
2 Tbsp / 25 ml orange dressing (page 200)	
1¼ cups / 300 ml chicken or vegetable stock (pages 194 and 206)	
salt and freshly milled pepper	
8 chive tops	

Serves 4

Shape a ¼-inch / .5-cm thick layer of Marbré de Canard around four of the quails' eggs and refrigerate for about 1 hour.

Thoroughly dry the spinach on a dish towel, then remove the stems and season the leaves. Wrap the pâté balls carefully in the spinach leaves. Garnish each one with two strips of egg white and one tomato diamond. Melt half the aspic and use to coat the pâté balls. Refrigerate the *pralines* until set. Repeat, if necessary, so they have a shiny coating.

Place one *praline* on each plate. Finely chop the remaining aspic and pipe a little around the bottom of each. Arrange three orange segments on each plate. Toss the assorted salad leaves in three-quarters of the dressing and place at the top of each plate.

Warm the remaining four quails' eggs in the chicken or vegetable stock and dip into the remaining dressing. Place one egg on each salad nest and garnish with chive tops.

SYMPHONIE DE CRUSTACES AUX OEUFS DE CAILLE

SHELLFISH AND QUAILS' EGGS IN ASPIC

Wash and open the oysters (page 199). Remove the beards. Bring ½ cup less 1 Tbsp/100 ml of the wine to a boil with the shallot. Drop in the oysters and as soon as the liquid returns to a boil, remove the oysters and place in ½ cup less 1 Tbsp/100 ml of chilled white wine to cool.

Poach and cool the scallop in the same way. When cold, dry the oysters and scallop thoroughly.

Melt the chicken aspic, then leave to cool. Coat the inside of four dariole molds (page 166) with a very thin layer of the aspic. Leave to set in the refrigerator or over a bowl of ice.

Dip the truffle, carrot, hard-boiled egg white, leek and eight of the tomato diamonds in a little aspic and arrange two of each in a star pattern on the base of each mold with a sprig of fresh dill in the center. Arrange oysters and sliced artichokes on the top of the vegetable diamonds. Pour in a little

4 fresh oysters, preferably natives if available
1½ cups/350 ml dry white wine
1 Tbsp/10 g chopped shallot
1 oz/25 g fresh scallop (white part only), cut in thin slices
1¾ cups/400 ml chicken aspic (page 193)
8 truffle diamonds
8 carrot diamonds
8 hard-boiled egg white diamonds
8 leek diamonds
28 plum tomato diamonds
24 sprigs of fresh dill
2 artichoke bottoms, trimmed and cut in ¼-inch/ .5-cm thick slices
4 medallions cooked lobster tail
4 cooked langoustine tails
1 Tbsp/10 g finely diced carrot, blanched
1⅓ Tbsp/10 g finely diced fennel, blanched
1½ Tbsp/10 g finely diced leek, blanched
4 quails' eggs, soft-boiled and shelled (page 207)
6-inch/15-cm piece of cucumber
¼ cup/50 ml white-wine vinegar
2 Tbsp/25 g superfine sugar
salt and freshly milled pepper

Serves 4

aspic to just cover and leave to set. Add a little more aspic and swirl around the inside of the molds.

Arrange the lobster medallions, langoustine tails, scallop, diced vegetables and quails' eggs neatly in the dariole molds, always lining them with a little aspic and leaving to set between each layer. Cover the last layer with aspic and leave to set in the refrigerator for at least 2 hours.

Canalé the cucumber and cut in very thin slices. Mix the remaining white wine, white-wine vinegar, sugar, salt and pepper, and marinate the cucumber slices for 10 minutes. Drain well. Dip the remaining tomato diamonds in the marinade, then drain well. Arrange a neat ring of cucumber slices on each plate.

Unmold a *symphonie de crustaces* in the center of each plate. Garnish with the remaining tomato diamonds and sprigs of dill.

TARTARE DE
SAUMON D'ECOSSE A L'ANETH

SALMON TARTARE

Dry the salmon on a dish towel. Mix the salt, sugar and saltpetre. Cover the salmon evenly with this mixture and leave for about 2½ hours. Wash and dry the salmon and leave in a cool place for about 6 hours.

To make the sauce, mix all the ingredients together and beat until the mixture becomes almost white. Stir in

14 oz/400 g fillet of wild salmon, skin and bones removed
4 Tbsp/50 g sea salt
1⅓ Tbsp/15 g superfine sugar
½ tsp/2.5 g saltpetre
juice of ½ lemon
salad greens
salt and freshly milled pepper
2 tsp/10 g Keta caviar
4 sprigs of dill
SAUCE
⅔ cup/150 ml mayonnaise (page 199)
2 Tbsp/25 ml white-wine vinegar
¼ cup/50 ml oil
2 tsp/10 g Dijon mustard
¼ cup/50 ml sugar syrup (page 204)
freshly chopped dill

Serves 4

freshly chopped dill to taste and season with salt and pepper.

Cut the salmon in small cubes and sprinkle with the lemon juice. Arrange the salad greens and some of the chilled salmon cubes on each plate.

Pour a little sauce around each portion and garnish with caviar and sprigs of dill.

SALADE SAINT-HUBERT

ST HUBERT'S SALAD

1 grouse, dressed	
1 partridge, dressed	
4 oz / 100 g fillet of venison	
½ cup less 1 Tbsp / 100 ml Madeira	
½ cup less 1 Tbsp / 100 ml Madeira sauce (page 198)	
3 oz / 75 g assorted salad leaves	
orange dressing (page 200)	
8 segments of blood orange (page 203)	
8 segments of orange	
8 segments of grapefruit	
1½ Tbsp / 25 g unsalted butter	
1 Tbsp / 10 g chopped shallot	
1 cup / 60 g chanterelles, cleaned	
freshly snipped chives	
1 oz / 25 g fresh foie gras, diced	
all-purpose flour	
2 Tbsp / 25 ml oil	
salt and freshly milled pepper	

Serves 4

Heat the oven to 425°F/220°C and roast the grouse for about 10 minutes, the partridge for about 8 minutes and the fillet of venison for about 4 minutes, after which cooking times all the meats will be still be very pink. Leave to rest for 10 minutes in a warm place. *Déglacé* the roasting pan with the Madeira, reduce and pass through a fine strainer, then add to the Madeira sauce.

Toss the assorted salad leaves in a little dressing until just glistening. Arrange some in the center of each plate with the orange and grapefruit segments around the edge of each portion.

Remove the breasts from the partridge and grouse and cut in thin slices. Cut the fillet of venison in thin slices. Arrange some slices of meat on each salad.

Melt the butter and sweat the shallot and chanterelles, season with salt and pepper, sprinkle with a few chopped chives and arrange on top of each portion.

Season the foie gras with salt and pepper and dust very lightly with flour. Heat the oil and very quickly toss the foie gras. Drain and add to the sauce at the last moment; serve this separately.

TERRINE D'AVOCAT
AUX CRABE ET TOMATES

AVOCADO TERRINE WITH CRAB
AND TOMATO

Blanch the spinach quickly in boiling salted water and refresh. Dry thoroughly and season with salt and pepper. Line a buttered 5-cup/1.25-liter terrine with the spinach leaves.

Cut each avocado in half, then remove the skin and seed. Reserve two halves and brush with a little lemon juice. Pass the remaining avocados through a fine strainer or blend in a food processor with a little lemon juice.

Warm the gelatin in the chicken stock until dissolved and add the avocado purée. Stir in the crab meat, horseradish and a dash of Tabasco sauce. Fold in the half-whipped cream and season to taste.

5 oz/150 g young spinach leaves
5 medium-sized avocados
juice of ½ lemon
¾ oz/20 g leaf gelatin, soaked in a little chicken stock or cold water
1 cup/125 g flaked white crab meat
1⅓ Tbsp/20 g freshly grated horseradish
Tabasco sauce
2¼ cups/500 ml heavy cream, half-whipped
salt and freshly milled pepper
4 Tbsp/50 g strips of plum tomato fillets
5 Tbsp/75 g Keta caviar
3⅓ Tbsp/50 g Beluga caviar
SAUCE
1¼ cups/300 ml mayonnaise (page 199)
2 Tbsp/25 ml white-wine vinegar
¼ cup/50 ml sugar syrup (page 204)
2 Tbsp/25 ml Aquavit
⅔ cup/150 ml heavy cream, whipped
2 Tbsp/10 g freshly snipped chives

Serves 10

Half-fill the lined terrine with the avocado mixture. Cut the reserved avocado in strips and lay along the center. Cover with the remaining avocado mixture. Fold over any spinach leaves which overlap and chill in the refrigerator for at least 4 hours.

To make the sauce, mix the mayonnaise with the vinegar, sugar syrup, Aquavit and Tabasco sauce to taste. Fold in the whipped cream. Add the snipped chives and season with salt and pepper.

Unmold the avocado terrine and cut in slices about ½-inch/1-cm thick. Position on individual plates and pour a little sauce around each portion. Garnish with tomato fillets and caviar.

VOL-AU-VENT FINANCIER A LA SAVOY

VOL-AU-VENT WITH KIDNEY AND SWEETBREADS

One of Carême's recipes, this is an example of classic French cooking. It was first made for a member of the Rothschild family – the word financier *in the title subtly suggests the association.*

Roll out the puff pastry dough about ¼-inch/.5-cm thick. Cut out four rectangles, each 2½ × 2-inches/6 × 5-cm. Mark the top of each rectangle with a knife about ¼-inch/.5-cm from the edge and mark a criss-cross pattern in the inner portion.

Place on a baking sheet, brush with beaten egg yolk and leave to rest for at least 20 minutes. Bake at 425°F/220°C for about 20 minutes until golden brown. Carefully remove the lid from each vol-au-vent and take out any uncooked dough inside the case.

Melt 2 Tbsp/25 g of the butter in a pan, season the kidneys with salt and

9 oz/250 g puff pastry dough (page 200)	
1 egg yolk, beaten	
½ cup/100 g unsalted butter	
9 oz/250 g veal kidney, fat removed and cut in cubes	
heaped 3 cups/225 g quartered button mushrooms	
¼ cup/50 ml truffle juice (page 198)	
¼ cup/50 ml ruby port	
¼ cup/50 ml Madeira	
1¾ cups/400 ml jus de veau (page 197)	
1⅓ Tbsp/10 g chopped truffles	
6 oz/175 g veal sweetbreads, blanched and cut in cubes	
¼ cup/50 g chicken mousse shaped into tiny quenelles (page 206)	
1½ oz/40 g fresh cocks' combs, prepared (page 197)	
salt and freshly milled pepper	
4 turned mushrooms (page 183)	
4 slices of truffle	

Serves 4

pepper and seal very quickly so that they still remain pink.

Melt 2 Tbsp/25 g of the butter and sweat the mushrooms. Season to taste and remove from the pan. Add the truffle juice, port and Madeira to the pan and reduce by two-thirds. Add the jus de veau and reduce to the desired consistency. Add the chopped truffle, kidneys, sweetbreads, mushrooms, chicken quenelles and cocks' combs. Season to taste and stir in 2 Tbsp/25 g of the butter.

Place a vol-au-vent on each plate and fill generously with the kidney mixture. Melt the remaining butter and brush the vol-au-vent lids with some, then sweat the turned mushrooms in the remaining butter and season to taste. Warm the slices of truffle. Garnish each vol-au-vent with a turned mushroom and a slice of truffle and position the lid.

ASPERGES
AU BEURRE BLANC

ASPARAGUS WITH BEURRE BLANC

Cook the asparagus in boiling salted water for 3–4 minutes until *al dente*, then refresh. Trim the asparagus to about 4-inches/10-cm long.

Cut the fillets of salmon and turbot in thin strips about ¾-inch/2-cm wide and 3-inches/7.5-cm long. Wrap the ends of half the asparagus in the salmon and half in the turbot. Warm very quickly in a little vegetable stock until the fish is just cooked. Drain well and

16 asparagus spears, peeled
¼ lb/100 g fillet of wild salmon, skin and bones removed
¼ lb/100 g fillet of turbot or sole, skin and bones removed
1¼ cups/300 ml vegetable stock (page 206)
4 Timbales d'Asperges (page 186)
1 cup less 2 Tbsp/200 ml beurre blanc with lemon (page 192)
12 plum tomato diamonds
1 Tbsp/15 g unsalted butter, melted
salt and freshly milled pepper
16 sprigs of chervil

Serves 4

dry on a dish towel.

Fan out four asparagus spears on each plate and position one timbale beside the asparagus spears. Warm the beurre blanc and spoon a little over the asparagus.

Season the tomato diamonds with salt and pepper and warm them in the melted butter. Garnish each portion with the tomato diamonds and sprigs of chervil.

OMELETTE ARNOLD BENNETT

ARNOLD BENNETT'S OMELET

Arnold Bennett, who wrote Imperial Palace *while he was staying at The Savoy, invented this omelet. He subsequently demanded that chefs made it for him wherever he traveled, so it has now become an international favorite. At The Savoy this omelet is always made with finnan haddock, a Scottish delicacy available in America only by mail order.*

Poach the haddock in the milk for about 3 minutes. Remove from the pan and flake the fish.

Beat the eggs, then add salt and pepper and half the haddock.

Heat an omelet pan, add a quarter of

10 oz / 300 g smoked haddock fillets
1¼ cups / 300 ml milk
12 eggs
2⅔ Tbsp / 40 g unsalted butter
1¼ cups / 300 ml Béchamel sauce (page 192)
5 Tbsp / 75 ml Hollandaise sauce (page 197)
¼ cup / 50 ml heavy cream, whipped
4 Tbsp / 20 g grated Parmesan cheese
salt and freshly milled pepper

Serves 4

the butter and swirl around the pan. Add a quarter of the egg mixture and cook very quickly, stirring constantly until the mixture is lightly set. Slide the omelet out on to a plate.

Mix the Béchamel and Hollandaise sauces together quickly. Add the remaining flaked haddock and carefully fold in the whipped cream. Cover the omelet completely with a quarter of the sauce. Sprinkle with a quarter of the Parmesan and glaze under a hot broiler.

Repeat with the remaining mixture to make three more omelets.

Serve immediately.

COQUILLES SAINT-JACQUES GRILLÉES SUR CHOU-RAVE, BEURRE AU CITRON VERT

**BROILED SCALLOPS WITH KOHLRABI
IN LIME BUTTER SAUCE**

Wash the scallops under cold running water and dry on a dish towel. Cut each one in half (page 195).

Reduce the cream, add the vegetable batons, season with salt and pepper and add the Gruyère at the last moment.

Place the shallot, peppercorns, lime juice and white wine in a pan and reduce. Add the vegetable stock and reduce again. Slowly work in ½ cup/ 100 g of the chilled butter but do not allow to boil again. Pass the sauce through a fine strainer or cheesecloth and season to taste.

10 fresh scallops, with 4 corals reserved
½ cup less 1 Tbsp/100 ml heavy cream
5 oz/150 g kohlrabi, cut in batons (page 189) and blanched
2½-inch/6-cm piece of zucchini, cut in batons (page 189), blanched
2 Tbsp/25 g grated Gruyère
1 Tbsp/10 g chopped shallot
12 peppercorns, crushed
2 Tbsp/25 ml fresh lime juice
¼ cup/50 ml dry white wine
½ cup less 1 Tbsp/100 ml vegetable stock (page 206)
⅔ cup/150 g unsalted butter, chilled and diced
all-purpose flour
salt and freshly milled pepper
4 sprigs of chervil
dried lobster eggs (page 207)

Serves 4

Season the scallops with salt and pepper, then dust each one lightly with flour. Mark a lattice design on each one with red-hot skewers. Melt the remaining butter and brush the scallops and corals, then broil very quickly on both sides to cook lightly.

Place the vegetable mixture in the center of each soup plate and glaze lightly under a hot broiler. Arrange the scallops and corals on top. Pour the sauce around the scallops and garnish with the sprigs of chervil. If wished, sprinkle a few dried lobster eggs on the sauce.

GATEAU DE CAROTTES ET GRUYERE

CARROT GATEAU WITH GRUYERE

1¾ cups/200 g packed grated carrots
2½ Tbsp/40 g unsalted butter
⅔ cup/100 g chopped potato
½ cup/50 g grated Gruyère
1½ eggs, beaten
4½ tsp/10 g sugar
12 baby carrots
12 baby turnips
½ cup less 1 Tbsp/100 ml vegetable stock (page 206)
1 cup less 2 Tbsp/200 ml tomato coulis (page 204)
salt and freshly milled pepper
4 sprigs of basil

Serves 4

Sweat the carrot in half the butter for about 4 minutes. Boil the potato, drain and pass through a fine strainer. Mix the carrot, potato, Gruyère and egg, and season with salt and pepper.

Dust four small buttered ramekins with flour. Fill the ramekins with the vegetable mixture and cover with plastic wrap. Steam for about 20 minutes.

Divide the remaining butter and the sugar between two small pans. Glaze the baby carrots in one and the baby turnips in the other. Season with salt and pepper. Add half the vegetable stock to each. Cover and cook slowly until *al dente*.

Warm the tomato coulis. Unmold a carrot gâteau onto each plate. Pour a little tomato coulis around it and position the carrots and turnips. Garnish each portion with a sprig of basil.

FEUILLETE AUX CHAMPIGNONS DE BOIS

WILD MUSHROOMS IN A PUFF PASTRY LEAF

Roll out the puff pastry dough ¼-inch/.5-cm thick and cut out four large mushroom shapes. Mark with a criss-cross pattern using the back of a knife. Place on a baking sheet, brush with egg yolk and leave to rest for at least 20 minutes in a cool place. Bake at 400°F/200°C for about 15 minutes until golden brown.

Poach the quenelles very gently in the simmering chicken stock for 8 minutes. Drain and dry on a dish towel.

Sweat the shallot in half the butter until transparent. Add the wild mushrooms to the shallot and sweat for a further 2 minutes. Season with salt and pepper and a sprinkling of herbs.

4½ oz/120 g puff pastry dough (page 200)
1 egg yolk, beaten
8 quenelles of game (page 196)
2¼ cups/500 ml chicken stock (page 194)
1 Tbsp/10 g chopped shallot
5 Tbsp/75 g unsalted butter
1 cup/75 g ceps, cleaned
1 cup/75 g chanterelles, cleaned
3 oz/75 g pied de mouton, cleaned
freshly chopped herbs such as tarragon, chervil and chives
¼ cup/50 ml ruby port
½ cup less 1 Tbsp/100 ml jus de veau (page 197)
1 Tbsp/10 g dried morels, soaked in cold water for at least 1 hour
4½-inch/11-cm piece of leek, cut in *paysanne*
salt and freshly milled pepper

Serves 4

Reduce the port, add the jus de veau, season with salt and pepper and stir in 1 Tbsp/15 g of the butter. Add the sauce to the mushrooms.

Drain and wash the morels thoroughly. Dry on a dish towel. Melt 1 Tbsp/15 g of the butter, sauté the morels and add to the sauce.

Sweat the leek *paysanne* in the remaining butter in a covered pan for about 2 minutes until tender. Season with salt and pepper.

Cut the puff pastry shapes in half. Place some leek *paysanne* on each base and position two game quenelles on top. Spoon some mushroom sauce over each one and top with a puff pastry lid.

RAVIOLI
A L'ANCIENNE

RAVIOLI WITH SHELLFISH FILLING

¼ lb/100 g beet noodle dough (page 199)
¼ lb/100g spinach noodle dough (page 200)
¼ lb/100 g noodle dough (page 199)
3¾ cups/400 g chicken mousse (page 206)
1 lb/450 g hen lobster, preferably Scottish, cooked for 5 minutes (page 207), shell removed
½ cup plus 1 Tbsp/120 g unsalted butter
1 egg, beaten
3 large fresh scallops, corals removed and cut in ⅛-inch/.3-cm slices
½ cup/65 g flaked white crab meat
2 Tbsp/20 g chopped shallot
12 peppercorns, crushed
½ cup less 1 Tbsp/100 ml dry white wine
½ cup less 1 Tbsp/100 ml chicken stock (page 194)
1 cup less 2 Tbsp/200 ml heavy cream
2 oz/50 g Roquefort, sieved
basil leaves, cut in *julienne*
½ clove of garlic, crushed
6 plum tomatoes, filleted and cut in small dice
8 beet *sulfrino* balls, cooked in boiling salted water
12 carrot *sulfrino* balls, cooked in boiling salted water
12 cucumber *sulfrino* balls, cooked in boiling salted water
salt and freshly milled pepper
4 sprigs of basil

Serves 4

Roll out each noodle dough very thinly and cut each piece in half. On one piece of the beet noodle dough position eight small mounds of chicken mousse at regular intervals.

Cut the lobster tail in six medallions. Melt 1 Tbsp/15 g of the butter and use to toss the medallions. Season to taste and place on top of the chicken mousse. Position a small amount of chicken mousse on top of the lobster. Brush the dough between the lobster with beaten egg and lay the other piece of beet noodle dough on top. Press the dough carefully around the filling to seal, then cut in neat squares with a ravioli cutter.

Dry the scallops on a dish towel and season with salt and pepper. Melt 1 Tbsp/15 g of the butter and use to toss the scallops.

Position eight small mounds of chicken mousse on one piece of the spinach noodle dough at regular intervals, then lay some scallops on top and position a small amount of chicken mousse on the scallops. Brush the dough between the scallops with beaten egg and lay the other piece of spinach noodle dough on top. Press the dough carefully around the filling to seal, then cut in neat squares with a ravioli cutter.

Add the white crab meat to the remaining chicken mousse and position eight small mounds at regular intervals on the noodle dough. Brush the dough between the mousse with beaten egg and lay the other piece of noodle dough on top. Press the dough carefully around the filling to seal, then cut in neat squares with a ravioli cutter.

Cook all the ravioli in boiling salted water with a dash of oil until *al dente*. Drain and refresh.

Sweat half the shallots in 1 Tbsp/15 g of the butter, add the peppercorns and white wine and reduce. Add the chicken stock and cream, and reduce to a thin sauce consistency. Add the Roquefort and season to taste. Stir in a little basil julienne.

Sweat the remaining shallots and garlic in 1 Tbsp/15 g of the butter until transparent. Add the tomato and simmer until all the liquid has evaporated. Season with salt and pepper.

Place a little tomato in the center of each plate. Melt ¼ cup/50 g of the butter and toss all the ravioli until warm. Season with salt and pepper and arrange around the diced tomato. Pour a small amount of sauce over each ravioli. Melt the remaining butter and toss the vegetable balls until warm. Garnish the ravioli with sprigs of basil and vegetable balls.

GATEAU DE FOIE BLOND MADAGASCAR

CHICKEN LIVER GATEAU WITH MADAGASCAN PEPPERCORN SAUCE

14 oz/400 g chicken livers, trimmed
2¼ cups/500 ml milk
2 eggs
1¾ cups/400 ml heavy cream
grated nutmeg
1 red-skinned eating apple
1 green-skinned eating apple
¼ cup/50 ml dry white wine
2⅔ Tbsp/20 g chopped onion
¼ cup/50 g unsalted butter
2 Tbsp/25 ml oil
24 peppercorns, crushed
½ cup less 1 Tbsp/100 ml chicken stock (page 194)
¼ cup/50 ml jus de veau (page 197)
green peppercorns
freshly chopped basil
salt and freshly milled pepper

Serves 4

Soak the chicken livers overnight in the milk. Drain, wash thoroughly and dry on a dish towel. Mince the chicken livers or purée in a food processor, then pass through a fine strainer. Add the eggs and half the cream, and mix well. Season with a little grated nutmeg, salt and pepper.

Line four small ramekins with plastic wrap, allowing a little to overhang. Fill with the liver mixture, fold over the plastic wrap to cover completely and leave to rest in the refrigerator for 30 minutes. Poach in a water bath at 400°F/200°C for about 15 minutes. Remove from the oven and leave to rest in a warm place for 10 minutes.

Cut each apple in ten wedges and turn each piece, leaving the skin on one side. Blanch the apples in the wine and refresh. Reserve the wine.

Sweat the onions in half the butter and the oil until transparent. Add the peppercorns and white wine, and reduce. Add the chicken stock, jus de veau and remaining cream. Reduce to the required consistency, then pass through a fine strainer or cheese cloth. Season to taste. Stir in the remaining butter and add a sprinkling of green peppercorns and a little chopped basil.

Unmold a chicken liver gâteau on to each plate.

Pour some sauce around each portion and garnish with turned apples.

PETIT SOUFFLE D'ASPERGES VERTES AU BEURRE DE CERFEUIL

ASPARAGUS SOUFFLE WITH CHERVIL BUTTER

5 Tbsp/75 g unsalted butter	
¼ cup/40 g all-purpose flour	
1¼ cups/300 ml milk	
5 egg yolks	
4 tsp/20 g grated Gruyère	
Dijon mustard	
8 thin asparagus spears, peeled	
cayenne	
¼ lb/100 g savory pie crust dough (page 201)	
3 egg whites	
2 tsp/10 g plum tomato fillets	
1¼ cups/300 ml beurre blanc (page 192)	
salt and freshly milled black pepper	
8 sprigs of chervil	

Serves 4

Melt ¼ cup/50 g of the butter in a saucepan, add the flour and make a roux. Bring the milk to a boil and slowly add to the roux, stirring constantly, to form a smooth sauce. Beat the egg yolks, add to the mixture and cook over a gentle heat for 3–4 minutes, stirring constantly. Add the Gruyère and mustard to taste.

Cook the asparagus in boiling salted water for 3–5 minutes until *al dente*, then refresh. Cut off the tips about 1½-inches/4-cm long. Chop the stems very finely and add to the sauce. Season with salt and cayenne.

Roll out the dough very thinly and use to line four buttered ramekins (about 3½-inches/9-cm diameter). Whisk the egg whites until very stiff and fold into the warm asparagus sauce with a metal spoon. Use to fill the lined ramekins. Bake at 400°F/200°C for about 25 minutes.

Melt the remaining butter and warm the asparagus tips and tomato fillets. Season to taste. Pour a little of the beurre blanc onto each plate. Unmold the soufflés and place one on each plate. Garnish with asparagus tips, tomato fillets and sprigs of chervil.

MOUSSELINE DE SAINT-JACQUES AUX PERLES D'ESTURGEON

SCALLOP MOUSSELINE WITH CAVIAR

Thoroughly wash and dry the scallop and sole. Season with salt and leave to rest in the refrigerator for at least 20 minutes. Wipe the fish dry again, then mince or work very finely in a food processor.

Set a small bowl in a bowl of ice. Pass the fish mixture through a fine strainer into the chilled bowl. Slowly add the egg white, then slowly stir in the cream, keeping the bowl over ice all the time. Add the egg yolk and season. The consistency should be almost runny at this stage. Leave to rest for 20–30 minutes in the refrigerator until the mousseline mixture becomes slightly firm.

Butter four timbale molds or egg cups and, using a teaspoon, half-fill with the mousseline mixture. Using a teaspoon, form a small cavity in each

2 oz/50 g fresh scallop (white part only)	
1 oz/25 g fillet of sole	
½ egg white	
½ cup less 1 Tbsp/100 ml heavy cream	
¼ egg yolk	
1⅔ Tbsp/25 g Beluga caviar	
salt	
12 chive tops	
SAUCE	
1 Tbsp/10 g chopped shallot	
18 peppercorns	
½ cup less 1 Tbsp/100 ml dry white wine	
2 tsp/10 ml white-wine vinegar	
2 tsp/10 ml heavy cream	
½ cup/100 g unsalted butter, chilled and diced	
cayenne	

Serves 4

mousseline by turning the timbale mold evenly. Fill each cavity with about one-fifth of the Beluga caviar, leaving a little caviar for the sauce. Fill to the rim with the remaining mousseline mixture. Wrap in plastic wrap and steam for exactly 8 minutes. Timing is of great importance in this recipe.

To make the sauce, place the shallots, peppercorns, white wine and white-wine vinegar in a saucepan and reduce. Add the cream and reduce again. Slowly work in the diced butter over a very gentle heat. Do not allow the sauce to boil again. Season with cayenne and salt.

Unmold the steamed mousselines onto individual plates. Add the remaining caviar to the sauce at the last moment and pour around the mousselines. Garnish with chive tops.

CASSOULET D'ESCARGOTS A L'ANIS

SNAIL CASSEROLE

Sweat the shallot, garlic and diced vegetables in the butter until transparent. Add the snails and chanterelles and flame with the Pernod. Remove the snails and chanterelles, and add the chicken and vegetable stocks. Reduce by half, then add the cream. Reduce again to the desired consistency. Return the snails and chanterelles to the sauce. Add a little freshly chopped fennel and season to taste. Divide the mixture between four small copper saucepans or ovenproof dishes.

1 Tbsp/10 g chopped shallot
½ clove of garlic, crushed
2 Tbsp/20 g diced zucchini
3 Tbsp/20 g diced carrot
3 Tbsp/20 g diced celery root
2⅔ Tbsp/20 g diced fennel
1⅓ Tbsp/20 g unsalted butter
48 prepared snails (page 207)
1½ cups/100 g chanterelles, cleaned
2 Tbsp/25 ml Pernod
½ cup less 1 Tbsp/100 ml chicken stock (page 194)
½ cup less 1 Tbsp/100 ml vegetable stock (page 206)
1 cup less 2 Tbsp/200 ml heavy cream
freshly chopped fennel
7 oz/200 g puff pastry dough (page 200)
1 egg yolk, beaten
salt and freshly milled pepper

Serves 4

Roll out the puff pastry dough about ⅛-inch/.3-cm thick. Stamp out circles about 1-inch/2.5-cm larger in diameter than the copper pans. Brush the edge of the puff pastry dough with egg yolk and use to cover the pans, pressing the egg-washed dough firmly to the sides of the pans. Garnish the "lids" with any puff pastry dough trimmings and brush with egg yolk. Leave to rest for 20 minutes. Bake at 425°F/220°C for 15–20 minutes until the pastry is golden brown.

HUITRES
A MA FACON

ANTON EDELMANN'S OYSTERS

Wash and open the oysters (page 199), reserve the juice, remove and reserve the beards.

Bring two-thirds of the Champagne to the boil and add the shallot and peppercorns. Drop the oysters into the Champagne, bring just to simmering and remove immediately from the pan. Transfer to the remaining cold Champagne and leave to cool.

Combine all the Champagne with the oyster beards and juice and reduce by half. Pass through a strainer. Add

24 fresh oysters, preferably natives if available
1¼ cups/300 ml Champagne
1 Tbsp/10 g chopped shallot
12 white peppercorns, crushed
1 cup less 2 Tbsp/200 ml heavy cream
1-inch/2.5-cm piece of carrot, cut in *julienne* and blanched
1-inch/2.5-cm piece of leek, cut in *julienne* and blanched
¼ cup/50 ml Hollandaise sauce (page 197)
cayenne
salt
2⅔ Tbsp/40 g Beluga caviar
4 Timbales de Betterave (page 182)

Serves 4

half the cream and reduce to the desired consistency.

Add the *julienne* of vegetables to the sauce. Whip the remaining cream and add to the sauce with the Hollandaise sauce. Season to taste with cayenne and salt.

Arrange six oysters in a circle and spoon a little sauce over each oyster. Place under a hot broiler until golden.

Garnish each oyster with a little caviar and position a timbale in the center of each plate.

LES
POTAGES

ESSENCE DE POT-AU-FEU CHURCHILL

WINSTON CHURCHILL'S CONSOMME

Sir Winston Churchill insisted this soup was always served at dinners of The Other Club, of which he was honorary founder. A statue of the distinguished statesman still stands in the Pinafore Room when The Other Club meet. Sir Winston often celebrated his birthday at The Savoy when he would occasionally enjoy two servings of his favorite soup.

Simmer ¾ lb/350 g of the shin of beef in the beef and chicken stocks for about 2 hours until tender. Add the chicken for the last 30 minutes of cooking time. Leave the meats to cool in the stock.

Coarsely grind the remaining shin of beef and mix with the chopped vegetables and egg whites. Add the cooled stock and mix well. Add the thyme, peppercorns, salt and pepper.

Slowly bring to a boil, stirring occasionally with a metal spoon. As soon as

14 oz/400 g shin of beef
3 cups/750 ml beef stock (page 192)
3 cups/750 ml chicken stock (page 194)
1 small chicken
4 tsp/20 g chopped onion
3⅔ Tbsp/25 g chopped leek
2⅓ Tbsp/25 g chopped celery
2½ Tbsp/25 g chopped carrot
2 egg whites
1 sprig of fresh thyme
12 white peppercorns
3 young leeks, cooked in stock
4½ oz/120 g celery root, turned and cooked in stock
4½-inch/11-cm piece of carrot, turned and cooked in stock
7¼-inch/18-cm piece of zucchini, turned and cooked in stock
3 oz/75 g Savoy cabbage balls (page 185)
4 × ¾-inch/2-cm pieces of marrow bone
½ bread flute
2½ oz/65 g meat marrow off the bone
4 Tbsp/20 g grated Parmesan
salt and freshly milled pepper

Serves 4

a froth forms on top of the stock, stop stirring and simmer over a very gentle heat for about 2 hours, then pass through fine cheesecloth. Season with salt and pepper.

Add the chicken and shin of beef to the consommé. Add the leeks, turned vegetables and Savoy cabbage balls to the soup.

Blanch the pieces of marrow bone for 2 minutes, scrape the bones clean with a knife, then add to the soup. Reheat gently.

Cut the bread flute in thin slices, toast and top with the raw marrow. Sprinkle with Parmesan and brown under a hot broiler.

Remove the chicken and beef from the saucepan and cut in slices. Cut the leeks in short lengths. Arrange some of the meat and leeks in each soup plate, ladle some consommé, vegetables and a piece of marrow bone on top and serve the toasted marrow separately.

CREME FINES HERBES
AUX QUENELLES DE STILTON

HERB SOUP WITH STILTON QUENELLES

¼ oz/10 g fresh herbs such as tarragon, fennel, chives, chervil and basil	*Serves 4*

Pick the herb leaves from their stems and chop finely. Reserve the stems.

Sweat the onion in the butter until transparent. Add the fennel, celery and leek to the onion. Sweat for a further 5 minutes. Add 4 cups/1 liter of the chicken stock, salt, pepper and herb stems, and simmer for about 20 minutes.

Purée, then pass through a strainer and return to the heat. Add the chopped herbs to the soup and simmer for

⅓ cup/65 g chopped onion

¼ cup/50 g unsalted butter

1¾ cups/200 g minced fennel

1⅔ cups/200 g minced celery

2½ cups/200 g minced leek, white part only

5½ cups/1.5 liters strong chicken stock (page 194)

½ cup less 1 Tbsp/100 ml heavy cream

scant 1 cup/200 g chicken mousse (page 206)

2 oz/50 g Stilton, cut in dice

small pieces of vegetables such as leeks and carrots, cut in *brunoise* and blanched

salt and freshly milled pepper

4 sprigs of basil

about 5 minutes. Beat in the cream and season to taste.

Mix the chicken mousse, Stilton and vegetable *brunoise* together and form into twelve quenelles.

Poach very gently for about 4 minutes in the remaining stock.

Place three quenelles in each soup plate and ladle some soup over each portion. Garnish with sprigs of basil and serve with croutons (page 195).

BISQUE DE LANGOUSTINE AUX RAVIOLI ET CONCOMBRE

LANGOUSTINE BISQUE WITH RAVIOLI AND CUCUMBER

Serves 4

2 Tbsp/25 ml oil
2¼ lb/1 kg langoustine shells, finely crushed (page 201)
scant 1¼ cups/120 g mirepoix (page 207)
½ clove of garlic, crushed
¼ cup/50 ml brandy
2⅔ Tbsp/40 g tomato paste
½ cup less 1 Tbsp/100 ml dry white wine
2¼ cups/500 ml chicken stock (page 194)
2¼ cups/500 ml fish stock (page 196)
1¾ cups/400 ml heavy cream
¼ lb/100 g noodle dough (page 199)
heaped 1 cup/120 g fish mousse (page 196)
12 cooked langoustine tails
¼ cup/50 g unsalted butter
1 egg yolk, beaten
1-inch/2.5 cm thick piece of cucumber, cut in *julienne*
salt and freshly milled pepper

Heat the oil and fry the langoustine shells very quickly. Add the mirepoix and garlic and fry for a further 2–3 minutes. Flame with half the brandy, then add the tomato paste. Add the white wine and chicken and fish stocks, and reduce by half. Stir in the cream and reduce to the required consistency. Pass through fine cheesecloth and season the bisque to taste.

Roll out the noodle dough very thinly and cut in half. Divide the fish mousse into eight portions and position four of these evenly spaced on one piece of the noodle dough.

Toss four of the langoustine tails in half the butter, season with salt and pepper, flame with the remaining brandy and place one on top of each portion of fish mousse. Cover with the remaining portions of fish mousse and brush the noodle dough with the egg yolk. Lay the other half of the noodle dough on top and press it carefully around the filling to seal it. Cut into four neat squares with a ravioli cutter. Cook the ravioli in boiling salted water with a dash of oil for 2 minutes.

Toss the cucumber *julienne* in the remaining butter. Warm the ravioli in the bisque with the cucumber *julienne* and remaining langoustine tails.

POTAGE DE MOULES ET POIREAUX AU THYM

MUSSEL AND LEEK SOUP

Serves 4

1¾ lb/750 g fresh mussels
2 cups/200 g white mirepoix (page 207)
½ clove of garlic
2 sprigs of lemon thyme, stems and leaves separated
1 cup less 2 Tbsp/200 ml dry white wine
½ cup/50 g finely diced fennel
½ cup/50 g finely diced carrot
2 cups/100 g finely chopped leek
4⅓ Tbsp/65 g unsalted butter
4 cups/1 liter strong chicken stock (page 194)
saffron strands
1 cup less 2 Tbsp/200 ml heavy cream
2 egg yolks
3⅔ Tbsp/50 g finely diced plum tomato fillets
cayenne
salt

Wash and scrub the mussels thoroughly under cold running water. Ensure they are all firmly closed.

Put the mirepoix, mussels, garlic, stems of lemon thyme and white wine into a large saucepan. Cover with a lid and cook for 3–5 minutes over a high heat, stirring frequently, until all the mussels have opened.

Strain through a colander into a large bowl, discarding any mussels that remain closed. Cover the mussels with a damp cloth to keep them moist. Place the mussel stock in a tall container tilted at a slight angle to allow any sand to settle. Carefully ladle off the stock from the top.

Remove the mussels from their shells and discard the beards. Sweat the diced vegetables in the butter, add the mussel stock, chicken stock and a generous pinch of saffron, and simmer for about 20 minutes until the vegetables are tender.

Mix the cream with the egg yolks and add some of the hot stock. Add this mixture to the soup and reheat, but do not boil again. Add the mussels, lemon thyme leaves and diced tomato. Season to taste with cayenne and salt.

Serve with warm toasted slices of bread flute.

CREME D'HUITRES AU PERNOD

OYSTER SOUP WITH PERNOD

12 fresh oysters, preferably natives
2½ oz/65 g young spinach leaves, blanched
½ cup less 1 Tbsp/100 ml dry white wine
2 Tbsp/25 ml Pernod
3 cups/750 ml chicken stock (page 194)
2 egg yolks
1 cup less 2 Tbsp/200 ml heavy cream
2 Tbsp/10 g sorrel, cut in *julienne*
¾-inch/2-cm piece of carrot, cut in *julienne* and blanched
1¼-inch/3-cm piece of leek, cut in *julienne* and blanched
1⅓ Tbsp/20 g unsalted butter

Serves 4

Wash and open the oysters (page 199). Reserve the juice, remove and reserve the beards.

Remove the stems and thoroughly dry the spinach on a dish towel. Wrap the oysters in the leaves. Bring the wine to a boil and cook the oysters for a few seconds. Remove from the pan. Add the Pernod, chicken stock and reserved oyster juice and beards to the wine. Simmer for 3–4 minutes, then pass through fine cheesecloth.

Mix the egg yolks with the cream and add the stock and vegetable *julienne*. Stir well over a low heat until thickened but do not boil again. Season with cayenne and salt.

Place three oysters in each soup plate and ladle some soup over each portion.

CREME D'OIGNONS AU PORTO

ONION SOUP WITH PORT

Sweat the onion in the butter until transparent. Add the fennel, leek, chicken stock, salt and pepper. Simmer slowly for about 25 minutes until all the ingredients are well cooked. Purée and pass through a fine

3¼ cups/550 g finely chopped onions
4⅓ Tbsp/65 g unsalted butter
¾ cup/75 g chopped fennel
1 cup/75 g chopped leek
4 cups/1 liter chicken stock (page 194)
½ cup less 1 Tbsp/100 ml heavy cream
¼ cup/50 ml ruby port
salt and freshly milled pepper

Serves 4–6

strainer. Return to the heat and stir in the cream. Add the port and season with salt and pepper.

Ladle the soup into soup plates and garnish with a spoonful of port, if liked. Serve with croutons (page 195).

ELIXIR DE CRUSTACES EN GELEE

CHILLED CONSOMME WITH SHELLFISH

1 lb/450 g live hen lobster, preferably Scottish

4 cups/1 liter vegetable stock (page 206)

4 live langoustines

4 live crayfish

2 fresh scallops, corals removed

½ cup less 1 Tbsp/100 ml dry white wine

⅔ cup/100 g boned chicken leg meat

1 egg white

2 Tbsp/20 g chopped celery

3 Tbsp/20 g chopped carrot

1½ Tbsp/10 g chopped onion

4 cups/1 liter chicken stock, chilled (page 194)

saffron strands

1½ Tbsp/15 g carrot diamonds, cooked in stock

1½ Tbsp/15 g turnip diamonds, cooked in stock

2 Tbsp/15 g leek diamonds, cooked in stock

1⅓ Tbsp/20 g plum tomato diamonds

salt and freshly milled pepper

Serves 4

Cook the lobster in the boiling vegetable stock for 5 minutes. Drain and refresh. Remove and reserve the shell. Cut the tail in eight medallions.

Cook the langoustines in the boiling vegetable stock for 3 minutes and the crayfish for 2 minutes. Drain and refresh. Remove and reserve the shells.

Cut each scallop in half. Season and poach for 1 minute in the white wine. Leave to cool.

Crush the lobster, langoustine and crayfish shells very finely. Coarsely grind the chicken leg meat. Mix the shells, chicken, egg white, celery, carrot and onion together. Add the chilled chicken stock, a pinch of saffron, salt and pepper, and mix well. Bring slowly to a boil, stirring occasionally with a metal spoon. As soon as a froth forms on top of the stock, stop stirring and simmer over a very gentle heat for 1½–2 hours. Pass carefully through very fine cheesecloth and season to taste. Chill the consommé until just syrupy.

Divide the lobster claws, medallions, scallops, langoustines, crayfish, vegetable and tomato diamonds between four soup plates and pour the chilled consommé over each portion.

ESSENCE DE CAILLE FUMÉE
AVEC PAILLETTES AU CARVI

SMOKED QUAIL CONSOMME WITH CARAWAY STRAWS

Remove the legs from the quails. Smoke the quail breasts in a hot smoker for 25 minutes. (The breasts are partially cooked in fresh smoke with simultaneous heating in a commercial smoker.) Take the quail breasts off the bone and reserve.

Chop the quails' legs and the smoked quail carcass, and mix with the mirepoix and egg white. Add the cold quail or chicken stock, peppercorns, thyme, bay leaf, salt and pepper. Bring slowly to a boil, stirring occasionally with a metal spoon. As soon as a froth forms on top of the stock, stop stirring and simmer over a gentle heat for about 1 hour. Pass through fine cheesecloth and season to taste.

Cook the vegetable *julienne* in a little of the quail or chicken consommé for about 2 minutes. Add a sprinkling of freshly chopped herbs to the stuffing, mix well and form into small quenelles using two teaspoons. Poach these in a little of the simmering consommé for about 2 minutes.

2 quails, dressed
scant 1/3 cup/40 g mirepoix (page 207)
1 egg white
5½ cups/1.5 liters quail or chicken stock (page 194)
12 peppercorns, crushed
1 sprig of thyme
½ bay leaf
½ cup/40 g carrot *julienne*
½ cup/40 g leek *julienne*
1/3 cup/40 g celery *julienne*
freshly chopped herbs
4 tsp/20 g stuffing for quail (page 201)
3 oz/75 g puff pastry dough (page 200)
1 egg yolk, beaten
2 Tbsp/10 g grated Parmesan
caraway seeds
paprika
4 quails' eggs, soft-boiled and shelled (page 207)
salt and freshly milled pepper
freshly snipped chives

Serves 4

Roll out the puff pastry dough about 1/8-inch/.3-cm thick. Brush with beaten egg yolk and sprinkle the dough evenly with the Parmesan, caraway seeds and paprika to taste. Stamp out four rings 1-inch/2.5-cm in diameter. Cut the remaining dough in long strips about ¼-inch/.5-cm wide. Roll each strip with your hands working in opposite directions to achieve a twisted straw effect.

Leave to rest for 20 minutes, then bake at 400°F/200°C for about 15 minutes.

Cut the caraway straws in 4-inch/10-cm long sticks and place four in each pastry ring.

Remove the skin from the smoked quail breasts and cut in slices. Warm the quails' eggs, *julienne* of vegetable and quenelles in the hot consommé. Arrange one quail breast in each soup plate and ladle some of the consommé over each portion. Garnish with freshly snipped chives. Serve the caraway straws separately.

LES POISSONS ET
LES CRUSTACES

TURBOT
POCHE AMIRAL

WHOLE POACHED TURBOT

8 lb / 3.5 kg turbot	
2 cups / 400 g fish mousse (page 196)	
2 tsp / 10 g raw lobster eggs	
8¾ cups / 2 liters fish stock (page 196)	
8¾ cups / 2 liters vegetable stock (page 206)	
5 Tbsp / 75 g unsalted butter	
4 cups / 1 liter white wine sauce (page 206)	
cayenne	
10 live crayfish	
10 small button mushrooms, turned	
juice of ½ lemon	
glace de viande (page 197)	
salt and freshly milled pepper	
10 fleurons (page 196)	

Serves 10

The culinary genius of Auguste Escoffier is still venerated by discerning gastronomes. The great chef created this dish when he was introducing the art of haute cuisine to London at the end of the last century. The frequent presence of the Prince of Wales no doubt encouraged society hostesses to start a new custom of entertaining in a public restaurant.

With a long, narrow filleting knife, make an incision at the head end of the backbone and then carefully work down the backbone easing the flesh away without perforating the skin. Turn the fish over and ease the flesh from the other side. Loosen the entire bone and carefully remove from the turbot. Shape ten quenelles from the fish mousse, using two teaspoons, and place on wax paper.

Pass the raw lobster eggs through a fine strainer and add three-quarters to the remaining fish mousse to color it. Reserve the remaining quarter for the lobster butter.

Carefully fill the boned-out turbot with the lobster-colored mousse. It should not be too full as the mousse will expand during poaching.

Place the turbot in a *turbotière* or a large roasting pan with the dark skin side on top. Season with salt and pepper. Pour in the fish and vegetable stocks. Cover with wax paper and braise at 300°F/150°C for about 1 hour, basting frequently with the stock. Remove the turbot from the pan, reserving the stock. Remove the dark skin very carefully and all the side fins. Dry the fish thoroughly with a dish towel and place on a large silver tray or serving dish.

Mix ¼ cup / 50 g of the butter with the reserved lobster eggs and chill.

Bring the white wine sauce to a boil, remove from the heat and work in the lobster butter. Season to taste with cayenne, salt and pepper.

Bring some of the reserved stock to a boil and cook the crayfish for 2 minutes, then refresh. With scissors, remove the under-shell from the crayfish tails and loosen the flesh, but do not remove.

Poach the fish quenelles in a little of the reserved stock.

Melt the remaining butter and toss the turned mushrooms. Add a dash of lemon juice to retain the color.

Arrange the quenelles and button mushrooms along the length of the turbot and pour the sauce carefully over the fish so that it is well covered. Warm the crayfish quickly and arrange around the turbot. Dot the mushrooms with *glace de viande*. Garnish with the fleurons.

AIGUILLETTES DE TRUITE SAUMONEE ET BARBUE GRILLEES A L'ANETH

BROILED SALMON TROUT AND BRILL

Cut the fillet of salmon trout in four equal pieces and the fillet of brill in eight equal pieces. Dry each piece on a dish towel. Season with salt and pepper. Dust lightly with flour and mark a lattice design with red-hot skewers on each piece of fish.

Cut the cucumber in ⅛-inch/.3-cm thick slices. Reduce the vegetable stock and cream to a very thick consistency. Add the cucumber slices and bring to a boil. Season with salt and pepper and add the diced tomato and a sprinkling of dill at the last moment.

Sweat the chopped onions in half the oil and 1 Tbsp/15 g of the butter until transparent. Add the peppercorns, white-wine vinegar and white

7 oz/200 g filiet of salmon trout, skin and bones removed
14 oz/400 g fillet of brill or sole, skin and bones removed
12-inch/30-cm piece of cucumber, pared, cut in half lengthwise and seeds removed
¼ cup/50 ml vegetable stock (page 206)
⅔ cup/150 ml heavy cream
2⅓ Tbsp/20 g diced plum tomato fillets
freshly chopped dill
½ cup/65 g minced onion
2 Tbsp/25 ml oil
¼ cup/50 g unsalted butter
60 peppercorns, crushed
2 Tbsp/25 ml white-wine vinegar
½ cup less 1 Tbsp/100 ml dry white wine
1 cup less 2 Tbsp/200 ml jus de veau (page 197)
salt and freshly milled pepper
4 sprigs of dill

Serves 4

wine, and reduce. Add the jus de veau and bring the sauce to a boil. Pass through a fine strainer, season to taste and stir in 1 Tbsp/15 g of the butter.

Melt the remaining butter, brush each piece of fish and cook under a moderate broiler for about 2½ minutes on each side.

Spoon a little cucumber mixture on to each plate. Arrange one piece of salmon trout and two pieces of brill beside it and pour some sauce between the pieces of fish. Garnish with a sprig of dill.

Note If salmon trout is not available, salmon may be substituted.

DELICE DE BARBUE BEATRICE

FILLET OF BRILL BEATRICE

10 oz / 300 g potatoes
2 egg yolks
4 × 4½-oz / 120-g portions of fillet of brill or sole, skin and bones removed
3⅔ Tbsp / 25 g all-purpose flour
⅔ cup / 150 g unsalted butter
¼ cup / 50 ml oil
8 fresh oysters, preferably natives if available
½ cup less 1 Tbsp / 100 ml dry white wine
heaped 2 cups / 120 g leek cut in *paysanne*
1 Tbsp / 10 g chopped shallot
12 white peppercorns, crushed
2 tsp / 10 ml lemon juice
¼ cup / 50 ml vegetable stock (page 206)
¼ cup / 50 ml fish stock (page 196)
2 Tbsp / 25 ml heavy cream
salt and freshly milled pepper
freshly snipped chives

Serves 4

Cut the potatoes on a mandolin in thin slices, then cut in *julienne*. Very quickly dip the potato *julienne* into a deep-fryer of hot oil and blanch them without coloring. Dry on a dish towel and season with salt and pepper. Mix with the egg yolks.

Season the fillets of fish with salt and pepper, dust with flour and cover one side with some of the potato mixture. Heat ¼ cup / 50 g of the butter and the oil and fry the pieces of fish until golden brown, cooking the potato-covered side first. Remove from the pan and keep warm.

Wash and open the oysters (see page 199). Remove and reserve the beards. Reserve four whole oysters and finely chop the remaining four. Quickly poach the whole oysters in the wine.

Cover and sweat the leeks in 2 Tbsp / 25 g of the butter for about 2 minutes until tender. Place the shallot, peppercorns, white wine and lemon juice in a saucepan and reduce. Add the vegetable and fish stocks and the oyster beards, and reduce. Add the cream and reduce to the required consistency. Remove from the heat and stir in the remaining butter. Season to taste, then pass through fine cheesecloth. Just before serving, stir in the chopped oysters.

Arrange a little of the leek on each plate and position a fillet of fish on top. Pour a little sauce around each fillet. Garnish each portion with a whole oyster and sprinkle with chives.

HADDOCK
FUME ALBAN

ALBAN'S SMOKED HADDOCK

4 × 4-oz/100-g portions of fillet of smoked haddock, bones removed
1¾ cups/400 ml milk
2 oz/50 g smoked haddock bones
½ cup less 1 Tbsp/100 ml dry white wine
1¾ cups/400 ml heavy cream
1 Tbsp/10 g chopped shallot
1⅓ Tbsp/20 g unsalted butter
½ clove of garlic, crushed
2 cups/300 g chopped plum tomato fillets
4 eggs, poached
6 oz/175 g new potatoes, turned and cooked
freshly chopped parsley
salt and freshly milled pepper

Serves 4

Poach the haddock portions in the milk for about 4 minutes.

Chop the haddock bones, place in a saucepan with the white wine, reduce and pass through a fine strainer of cheesecloth. Add the cream to the haddock reduction and reduce to the required consistency. Do not season the cream sauce as the haddock has a high salt content.

Sweat the shallot in half the butter until transparent, add the garlic and sweat for a further 30 seconds. Add the chopped tomato and simmer until all the liquid has evaporated. Season with salt and pepper.

Spoon some of the tomato mixture on to each plate and top with a portion of the haddock.

Warm the poached eggs in simmering salted water, then dry on a dish towel. Position a poached egg on each plate and spoon a little sauce over each egg and portion of fish.

Melt the remaining butter and toss the potatoes to warm, sprinkle with a little chopped parsley and position on the plates.

DELICE DE LOTTE A L'ORANGE

MONKFISH WITH ORANGE SAUCE

8 × 2½-oz/65-g portions of fillet of monkfish
heaped 1 cup/120 g lobster mousse (page 197)
8 large round lettuce leaves
⅔ cup/150 ml orange juice
1 cup less 2 Tbsp/200 ml white wine sauce (page 206)
2⅔ Tbsp/40 g unsalted butter
16 orange segments (page 203)
12 green peppercorns
¼ lb/100 g beet noodle dough (page 199), cooked
salt and freshly milled pepper
12 chive tops

Serves 4

Dry the monkfish on a dish towel and season with salt and pepper. Top each portion of monkfish evenly with some of the lobster mousse.

Blanch the lettuce leaves in boiling salted water for about 5 seconds and refresh. Dry the leaves on a dish towel and discard the stems. Use to wrap the portions of monkfish. Wrap in plastic wrap and steam for about 8 minutes.

Reduce the orange juice by two-thirds, add the white wine sauce and season to taste. Stir in half the butter.

Add the orange segments and green peppercorns to the sauce.

Toss the beet noodles in the remaining butter and season with salt and pepper. Arrange some of the noodles in a spiral at the top of each plate.

Remove the plastic wrap from the monkfish and position two portions on each plate.

Cover with some of the orange sauce and orange segments. Garnish with chive tops.

MARIAGE DE POISSON
A L'INDIENNE

**MARRIAGE OF FISH WITH
A CURRY SAUCE**

Carefully remove the scales, then remove any small bones from the red mullet and fillet of salmon with tweezers. Remove the skin from the fillet of salmon and reserve. Cut each scallop in half. Cut the fillet of salmon in strips of the same depth as the scallops and wrap one strip around each piece of scallop. Cut the salmon skin to the same depth as the fillet of salmon and wrap around each piece. Season with salt and pepper.

Mix the fish mousse with a generous sprinkling of fresh herbs, green peppercorns and crab meat. Season generously. Pipe the mixture into a length of sausage casing and tie in link sausages, about 3-inches/7.5-cm long. Simmer in salted water for about 8 minutes. Leave to rest in the refrigerator for at least 4 hours, then remove the casing.

Mark a lattice design with red-hot skewers on each sausage, then warm them in a well-buttered ovenproof dish at 275°F/140°C for 10 minutes.

2 medium-sized imported red mullet, filleted
5 oz/150 g fillet of salmon
2 fresh scallops, corals removed
1¼ cups/250 g fish mousse (page 196)
freshly chopped herbs
24 green peppercorns, crushed
1 Tbsp/10 g flaked white crab meat
a piece of sausage casing
¼ cup/50 ml oil
5 Tbsp/75 g unsalted butter
2 Tbsp/10 g chopped onion
½ clove of garlic, chopped
2 tsp/10 g curry powder
1 Tbsp/20 g chopped plum tomato fillets
mango chutney
4 tsp/20 g chopped apple
4 tsp/20 g chopped pineapple
1¼ cups/300 ml chicken stock (page 194)
¼ cup/50 ml white wine sauce (page 206)
¼ cup/50 ml heavy cream
¼ lb/100 g vegetables such as carrot, kohlrabi and zucchini, cut in "spaghetti" and blanched
salt and freshly milled pepper

Serves 4

Heat half the oil and 2 Tbsp/25 g of the butter and fry the salmon-wrapped scallops on both sides until golden brown.

Season the red mullet with salt and pepper and wrap in plastic wrap. Steam for 4 minutes.

Sweat the onions in the remaining oil and 2 Tbsp/25 g of the butter until transparent, add the garlic and sweat for a further 30 seconds. Add the curry powder and sweat for 30 seconds. Add the tomato, a spoonful of mango chutney, the apple, pineapple and the chicken stock, and simmer for about 20 minutes. Purée, then pass through a fine strainer. Reduce by two-thirds, add the white wine sauce and heavy cream, and season to taste.

Toss the vegetable "spaghetti" in the remaining butter and arrange some on each plate. Position a salmon-wrapped scallop on top and arrange the red mullet and a fish sausage on either side. Pour a little sauce around each portion.

DELICE DE TURBOT AU PAMPLEMOUSSE

TURBOT WITH PINK GRAPEFRUIT

Dust the portions of fish with a little flour and mark a lattice design with red-hot skewers. Melt 2 Tbsp/25 g of the butter and brush the fish, season with salt and pepper and cook under a moderate broiler, design-side down, for 4 minutes. Turn each portion over and brush with more melted butter, then cook for a further 4 minutes.

Place the stocks, crushed peppercorns, shallot, Sauternes and grapefruit juice in a saucepan and reduce by half. Add the cream and reduce by half. Stir in the remaining butter, reserving 1 Tbsp/15 g. Pass through a fine strainer and season to taste.

Warm the asparagus quickly in the vegetable stock, then toss in the reserved butter and season. Warm the grapefruit segments under a moderate broiler.

Position a portion of fish on each plate, garnish with asparagus tips and grapefruit segments, pour a little sauce beside each portion and sprinkle with a few lobster eggs, if wished.

4 × 5-oz/150-g portions of fillet of turbot or sole, skin and bones removed
all-purpose flour
⅔ cup/150 g unsalted butter
¼ cup/50 ml fish stock (page 196)
¼ cup/50 ml vegetable stock (page 206)
12 peppercorns, crushed
1 Tbsp/10 g chopped shallot
¼ cup/50 ml Sauternes
¼ cup/50 ml pink grapefruit juice
2 Tbsp/25 ml heavy cream
16 green asparagus tips, blanched
12 segments of pink grapefruit
salt and freshly milled pepper
dried lobster eggs (page 207), optional

Serves 4

FILET DE SAUMON BRAISE AU ROQUEFORT ET CELERI

BRAISED SALMON WITH ROQUEFORT AND CELERY

Season the portions of salmon with salt and pepper. Mix the fish mousse and the herbs, and pass through a fine strainer. Spread a thin layer of the mousse on top of each portion of salmon. Wrap in plastic wrap and steam for about 6 minutes.

Remove the plastic wrap and then sprinkle bread crumbs over each portion of salmon. Dot each with 1 Tbsp/15 g of the butter and brown

4 × 5-oz/150-g portions of fillet of salmon, skin and bones removed

¾ cup/150 g fish mousse (page 196)

8 Tbsp/20 g finely chopped fresh herbs such as chervil and tarragon

½ cup/50 g fresh white bread crumbs

5 Tbsp/75 g unsalted butter

3 Tbsp/10 g chopped celery leaves

1¼ cups/300 ml white wine sauce (page 206)

1 packed Tbsp/20 g sieved Roquefort cheese

1 Tbsp/10 g celery cut in *julienne*, blanched

salt and freshly milled pepper

4 sprigs of celery leaf, deep-fried (page 207)

4 fleurons (page 196)

Serves 4

under a moderate broiler.

Sweat the chopped celery leaves in the remaining butter, add the white sauce and simmer for about 10 minutes. Purée and pass through a fine strainer. Add the Roquefort and celery *julienne* to the sauce.

Pour a little sauce onto each plate and position a portion of salmon on top. Garnish with deep-fried celery leaves and fleurons.

PAUPIETTES DE SOLE FARCIES D'HOMARD

SOLE PACKAGES WITH LOBSTER STUFFING

Dry the fillets of sole on a dish towel and score the skin side with a small knife. Place between two sheets of plastic wrap and beat lightly. Season each fillet with salt and pepper. Spread a thin layer of lobster mousse onto each fillet of sole and cover the skin side with a layer of dry spinach leaves, then a thin layer of lobster mousse.

Cook the lobster in the boiling vegetable stock for about 5 minutes. Refresh and remove the shell carefully so that the tail and claws remain whole. Cut the lobster tail lengthwise in quarters and use with the knuckles to fill the center of the sole fillets. Roll each one carefully, wrap in plastic wrap and steam for about 8 minutes.

8 small quarter fillets of sole, skinned and trimmed
heaped ½ cup/120 g lobster mousse (page 197)
5 oz/150 g young spinach leaves, blanched and dried
1 lb/450 g live hen lobster, preferably Scottish
4 cups/1 liter vegetable stock (page 206)
7 oz/200 g vegetables such as carrot, leek and celery root, cut in *paysanne*
4⅓ Tbsp/65 g unsalted butter
¼ cup/50 ml dry sherry
1 cup less 2 Tbsp/200 ml lobster sauce (page 198)
2 Tbsp/25 ml oz brandy
1½ Tbsp/15 g dried morels, soaked in cold water for 2 hours
salt and freshly milled pepper
2 cooked lobster claws
4 fleurons (page 196)
dried lobster eggs (page 207), optional

Serves 4

Sweat the vegetable *paysanne* in 2 Tbsp/25 g of the butter in a covered saucepan. Season and arrange a little on each plate. Remove the plastic wrap from the *paupiettes* of sole and cut each one in three slices. Arrange on the vegetables.

Reduce the sherry, add the lobster sauce and brandy, and season to taste. Stir in 2 Tbsp/25 g of the butter. Pour a little sauce around the *paupiettes*.

Drain the morels and toss in the remaining butter, season and arrange on the sauce. Warm all the lobster claws in a steamer.

Garnish the *paupiettes* with lobster claws, fleurons and dried lobster eggs.

LOUP DE MER
AU CHAMPAGNE EN GONDOLE

SEA BASS POACHED IN PINK CHAMPAGNE

1 × 3 lb/1.5 kg sea bass
60 black peppercorns, very finely crushed
1 cup less 2 Tbsp/200 ml fish stock (page 196)
1 cup less 2 Tbsp/200 ml vegetable stock (page 206)
½ cup less 1 Tbsp/100 ml pink Champagne
12 fresh oysters, preferably natives if available
1 Tbsp/10 g chopped shallot
2 Tbsp/25 ml heavy cream
⅔ cup/150 g unsalted butter, chilled and diced
small bunch of fresh chives, snipped
cayenne
salt and freshly milled pepper
4 fleurons (page 196)

Serves 4

Open the sea bass by cutting carefully down both sides of the spine. Remove the spine with scissors without damaging the head, tail or belly of the fish. Discard the intestines and wash the body cavity thoroughly. Carefully pull out any small bones with tweezers. Dry the sea bass on a dish towel.

Place the fish in a buttered ovenproof dish, then season with salt and sprinkle generously with the crushed black peppercorns. Pour in the fish and vegetable stocks and Champagne. Cover and poach at 350°F/180°C for 12–15 minutes.

Remove the sea bass from the dish and keep covered in a warm place.

Reserve the cooking liquid.

Wash and open the oysters. Remove and reserve the beards. Drop the oysters into the cooking liquid for 5 seconds and remove. Keep warm. Add the oyster beards and the shallot to the cooking liquid and reduce. Add the cream and reduce to the required consistency. Remove from the heat and slowly work in the chilled butter. Pass through a fine strainer, but do not boil again. Season to taste. Add the freshly chopped chives and the oysters at the last moment.

Place the sea bass on a serving dish and spoon over the sauce. Garnish with the fleurons.

DELICE DE FLETAN AUX POMMES VERTES

HALIBUT WITH APPLE	1¼ lb/550 g fillet of halibut, skin and bones removed	Serves 4

Dry the fillet of halibut on a dish towel, then cut in twelve even slices.

Reserve eight apple quarters, then cut the remainder in small dice. Place a small knob of the butter and the sugar in a pan and melt over a medium heat. Add the apples and 2 Tbsp/25 ml of the cider. Cover with a piece of wax paper and stew very slowly until the apples are soft and the liquid has evaporated. Add half of the basil *julienne*.

Poach the reserved apple quarters in the sugar syrup for about 1 minute. Drain and place on a baking sheet. Brown under a hot broiler.

Canalé the carrots and cut in ⅛-inch/.3-cm thick slices. Blanch in boiling salted water, then toss in 1 Tbsp/15 g of the butter. Season with salt and pepper.

Ingredients:

- 8 eating apples, peeled, cored and quartered
- 5 Tbsp/75 g unsalted butter
- 4 tsp/20 g superfine sugar
- 1 cup less 2 Tbsp/200 ml dry cider
- 24 fresh basil leaves, cut in *julienne*
- 1 cup less 2 Tbsp/200 ml sugar syrup (page 204)
- 7 oz/200 g young carrots
- 1 Tbsp/10 g chopped shallot
- 12 peppercorns, crushed
- ½ cup less 1 Tbsp/100 ml vegetable stock (page 206)
- ½ cup less 1 Tbsp/100 ml fish stock (page 196)
- 1¼ cups/300 ml heavy cream
- cayenne
- all-purpose flour
- salt and freshly milled pepper
- 4 large sprigs of basil, deep-fried (page 207)

Place the shallots, peppercorns, remaining cider and vegetable and fish stocks in a saucepan and reduce. Add the cream and reduce to the required consistency. Season with cayenne and salt. Pass through a fine strainer or cheesecloth and stir in 2 Tbsp/25 g of the butter.

Season the halibut fillets, then dust with flour and sprinkle with the remaining basil *julienne*. Heat the remaining butter and the oil in a skillet and cook the pieces of halibut until golden brown on both sides.

Place a 2-inch/5-cm ring on a plate and fill it to about ½-inch/1-cm depth with the stewed apple. Repeat three times. Pour a little sauce on to each plate and arrange three pieces of halibut on top. Garnish with apple quarters, carrots and sprigs of basil.

ARLEQUINE DE CRUSTACES ET SA QUENELLE

SHELLFISH IN SAFFRON SAUCE WITH LOBSTER QUENELLE

1 lb/450 g live hen lobster
4 cups/1 liter vegetable stock (page 206), boiling
4 live langoustines
8 live crayfish
heaped ½ cup/120 g lobster mousse (page 197)
½ cup less 1 Tbsp/100 ml fish stock (page 196)
½ cup less 1 Tbsp/100 ml vegetable stock (page 206)
2 fresh scallops, corals removed
½ cup less 1 Tbsp/100 ml Noilly Prat
2½ Tbsp/20 g carrot diamonds
3 Tbsp/20 g leek diamonds
¼ cup/50 g unsalted butter
1 Tbsp/10 g chopped shallot
12 peppercorns, crushed
1 cup less 2 Tbsp/200 ml heavy cream
saffron strands
salt and freshly milled pepper
⅓ cup/65 g grapes, peeled

Serves 4

Cook the lobster in the boiling vegetable stock for 5 minutes. Drain and refresh. Cook the langoustines in the boiling vegetable stock for 3 minutes. Drain and refresh. Cook the crayfish in the boiling vegetable stock for 2 minutes. Drain and refresh.

Remove the shell from the lobster and cut the lobster tail in medallions. Remove the shells from the langoustines and the crayfish, then trim the tails (page 204).

Shape the lobster mousse into four quenelles and gently poach in the fish and vegetable stocks for about 5 minutes. Remove from the pan and dry on a dish towel.

Cut the scallops in half and season with salt and pepper. Bring the Noilly Prat to a boil and blanch the scallops very quickly.

Sweat the vegetable diamonds in half the butter in a covered pan until tender. Reduce the Noilly Prat with the fish and vegetable stocks, shallot and peppercorns. Pass through fine cheesecloth. Reduce the cream with a generous pinch of saffron strands and stir in the reduced stock. Add the vegetable diamonds, season to taste and stir in the remaining butter.

Warm the pieces of lobster, langoustines and crayfish very quickly in the sauce, then add the quenelles and scallops. Ladle into four soup plates and garnish with the warmed grapes.

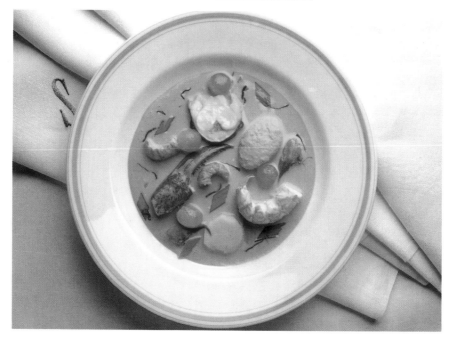

HOMARD BELUGA

LOBSTER WITH CAVIAR		*Serves 4*

4 × 1 lb/450 g live hen lobsters, preferably Scottish

4 cups/1 liter vegetable stock (page 206)

1 egg white

scant ⅓ cup/40 g mirepoix (page 207)

⅔ cup/100 g finely chopped plum tomato fillets

4 cups/1 liter strong chicken stock (page 194)

24 peppercorns, crushed

1 sprig of fresh thyme

2 cups/100 g leek diamonds

⅔ cup/100 g carrot diamonds

1½ oz/40 g young spinach leaves

2⅔ Tbsp/40 g Beluga caviar

8 long fresh chives

salt and freshly milled pepper

1⅓ Tbsp/10 g truffle *julienne*

Cook the lobsters one at a time in the boiling vegetable stock for 5 minutes. Drain and refresh. Carefully remove the shells, keeping the tails and claws whole (page 202).

Crush the lobster shells very finely (page 201) and mix with the egg white, mirepoix and chopped tomatoes. Mix in the cold chicken stock. Add the peppercorns, a sprig of fresh thyme, salt and pepper. Bring the stock slowly to a boil, stirring frequently with a metal spoon. As soon as a froth forms on top of the stock, stop stirring, and simmer over a very gentle heat for 1 hour. Pass through fine cheesecloth.

Cook the vegetable diamonds in a small amount of lobster consommé. Blanch the spinach leaves for 10 seconds in boiling salted water. Drain and refresh, then dry on a dish towel.

Overlap the spinach leaves to form eight small squares and spoon a little caviar onto each square. Fold over the leaves to form eight small, neat packages. Tie each package with a fresh chive and finish with a decorative bow.

Cut the lobster tails in half and warm them very quickly with the lobster claws and knuckles in the consommé. Add the vegetable diamonds.

Pour the consommé into four soup plates. Add two caviar packages to each portion and garnish with truffle *julienne.*

BROCHETTES DE LANGOUSTINE DIANA

SKEWERED LANGOUSTINES DIANA

1 lb/450 g medium-sized zucchini
24–32 cooked langoustine tails
¼ cup/50 ml olive oil
¼ cup/50 g unsalted butter
7 oz/200 g noodles (page 199)
⅔ cup/150 ml tomato coulis (page 204)
salt and freshly milled pepper

Serves 4

Peel two of the zucchini and cut the skin in long strips (discard the centers of these zucchini). Blanch the strips in boiling salted water and refresh. Cut the remaining zucchini in long, paper-thin slices. Season the zucchini with salt and pepper.

Wrap each langoustine in a slice of zucchini and thread six to eight on to each skewer. Fry in the oil and half the butter until golden brown.

Toss the noodles and zucchini strips in the remaining butter. Season and arrange in the center of each plate.

Warm the tomato coulis. Position the langoustines on top of the noodles and pour some of the coulis around each portion.

MEDAILLONS D'HOMARD D'ECOSSE
AUX GINGEMBRE ET OIGNONS VERTS

LOBSTER MEDALLIONS WITH GINGER AND SCALLIONS

Cook the lobsters one at a time in the boiling vegetable stock for 5 minutes. Drain and refresh. Carefully remove the shells so that the tails and claws remain whole.

Cut four of the scallions in fine *julienne* and blanch. Blanch twelve of the scallions until tender and tie in knots. Cut the remaining scallions in *paysanne* and sweat in 2 Tbsp/25 g of the butter in a covered saucepan for about 3 minutes until tender. Season with salt and pepper.

Reduce the Sauternes, then add the white wine sauce and ginger root. Pass through fine cheesecloth. Add the *julienne* of scallions to the sauce and

4 × 1 lb/450 g live hen lobsters, preferably Scottish
4 cups/1 liter vegetable stock (page 206)
30 scallions
5 Tbsp/75 g unsalted butter
½ cup/100 ml Sauternes
1¾ cups/400 ml white wine sauce (page 206)
1-inch/2.5-cm piece of ginger root, finely grated
4 Timbales de Broccoli (page 180)
12 pearl onions, cooked in salted water
1½ oz/40 g beet, turned and cooked in salted water
1½-inch/4-cm piece of cucumber, turned and cooked in salted water
salt and freshly milled pepper
dried lobster eggs (page 207), optional

Serves 4

stir in 2 Tbsp/25 g of the butter.

Place a little of the scallion *paysanne* on each plate.

Warm the lobsters quickly in the sauce. Cut each lobster tail in medallions, then re-assemble in sequence on top of the scallion *paysanne*.

Arrange the claws and knuckles around the medallions and spoon a little sauce over each portion. Unmold the timbales and position one on each plate. Warm the pearl onions, beet, cucumber and scallion knots in the remaining butter and use to garnish each portion.

Sprinkle with dried lobster eggs, if wished.

PETIT GATEAU
DE CRABE BOSTON

BOSTON CRAB MOUSSE

1 live large king crab	
½ egg white	
1¼ cups / 300 ml heavy cream	
½ egg yolk	
4 cups / 1 liter vegetable stock (page 206)	
cooked small crab claws (optional)	
⅓ average green pepper	
¹⁄₁₀ average red pepper	
1 corn-on-the-cob	
¼ cup / 50 g unsalted butter	
2 Tbsp / 25 ml oz brandy	
1 Tbsp / 10 g chopped shallot	
½ cup less 1 Tbsp / 100 ml dry white wine	
½ cup less 1 Tbsp / 100 ml chicken stock (page 194)	
salt and freshly milled pepper	

Serves 4

This dish has been in The Savoy repertoire for many years. Its title acknowledges the special American connection that has existed since the hotel first opened in 1889. Shellfish is abundant along the New England coast but Bostonians may not be familiar with this method of serving crab.

Kill the crab by plunging in boiling water for 1 minute and then refresh.

Remove one large claw from the crab. Crack the shell and remove all the meat from the claw. Pass it through a fine strainer into a bowl set over ice. Keeping the bowl over the ice, add the egg white slowly, stirring constantly. Slowly beat in ½ cup less 1 Tbsp/ 100 ml of the cream, then add the egg yolk and season the *mousseline* generously with salt and pepper.

Cook the crab in the boiling vegetable stock for 15 minutes. Remove and refresh.

Crack the shell and remove all the white crab meat from the remaining large claw and the small claws, taking care that no shells remain in the meat.

Add 2 tsp/10 g of the white crab meat to the crab *mousseline*. Butter four 4-inch/10-cm wide and ¾-inch/2-cm deep molds. If wished, place a cooked crab claw in each mold. Divide the crab *mousseline* between the molds and cover with plastic wrap. Steam for about 6 minutes.

Reserve about one-third of the green pepper. Blanch the red and remaining green pepper separately in boiling salted water for 30 seconds, then drain and refresh. Peel off the skins and cut the peppers in small dice.

Blanch the corn-on-the-cob in boiling salted water for 6 minutes. Remove the kernels from the cob. Drain and refresh.

Reduce ½ cup less 1 Tbsp/100 ml of the cream by half. Sweat the remaining white crab meat, all the diced green pepper, about two-thirds of the diced red pepper and the corn kernels in 1 Tbsp/15 g of the butter. Flame with the brandy and add the cream. Season with salt and pepper.

Cut the reserved green pepper in *brunoise*. Sweat the shallot in 1 Tbsp/ 15 g of the butter until transparent. Add the green pepper and sweat in a covered saucepan for 2 minutes. Add the white wine and chicken stock and cook until the green pepper is tender. Add the remaining cream and simmer for a further 3–4 minutes, then purée in a blender or food processor. Pass through a fine strainer, return to the heat and reduce to the required consistency. Season with salt and pepper and stir in 1 Tbsp/15 g of the butter.

Place a little of the creamed crab meat in the center of each plate. Unmold a crab *mousseline* on top. Pour a little green pepper sauce around each portion. Toss the reserved red pepper in the remaining butter until warm and use to garnish the sauce.

POT-POURRI DE
QUENELLES DE PECHEUR

POT-POURRI OF FISH QUENELLES

Divide the fish mousse in two equal portions. Bring half the cream to a boil, add a generous pinch of saffron strands and boil until very thick. Leave to cool, then pass through cheesecloth onto one portion of fish mousse. Mix well.

Shape four medium-sized quenelles from each portion of fish mousse. Repeat with the lobster mousse. Poach all the quenelles in the well seasoned vegetable stock for about 6 minutes, making sure that the stock never boils after it has been poured over the quenelles.

Sweat half the shallot in 2 Tbsp/25 g of the butter. Add the watercress and sweat, then add the white wine and reduce. Add half the white wine sauce and simmer for about 1 minute, then purée. Pass through a fine strainer or cheesecloth. Reduce to the required consistency, season to taste and stir in 1 Tbsp/15 g of the butter.

1¾ cups/350 g fish mousse (page 196)
½ cup less 1 Tbsp/100 ml heavy cream
saffron strands
1½ cups/175 g lobster mousse (page 197)
2¼ cups/500 ml vegetable stock (page 206)
1 Tbsp/10 g chopped shallot
5 Tbsp/75 g unsalted butter
3 cups/100 g roughly chopped watercress
¼ cup/50 ml dry white wine
1¼ cups/300 ml white wine sauce (page 206)
¼ cup/50 ml Noilly Prat
½ cup/40 g chanterelles, cleaned
2 Tbsp/25 ml olive oil
¼ lb/100 g young spinach leaves
salt and freshly milled pepper
½ cup less 1 Tbsp/100 ml lobster sauce (page 198)
4 fleurons (page 196)

Serves 4

Place the Noilly Prat and a pinch of saffron in a saucepan and warm to dissolve. Add the remaining white wine sauce and simmer for about 1 minute. Pass through a fine strainer or cheesecloth. Reduce to the required consistency, season to taste and stir in 1 Tbsp/15 g of the butter.

Sweat the remaining shallot in the remaining butter until transparent. Add the chanterelles and sweat for about 1 minute. Season to taste.

Heat the oil and toss the spinach leaves very quickly. Season with salt and pepper and arrange a few on each plate. Arrange three quenelles beside each portion of spinach. Spoon a little lobster sauce over each saffron quenelle, a little saffron sauce over each fish mousse quenelle and a little watercress sauce over each lobster quenelle. Garnish with chanterelles and fleurons.

LES VIANDES, LES VOLAILLES ET LE GIBIER

PAUPIETTES
DE VEAU VITTORIO

VEAL VITTORIO

This dish has recently been named after Vittorio, who is the butcher in The Savoy kitchens. He shares the record for long service with Maurice, for whom Perdreau braisé aux marrons Maurice *has been named.*

Cut the fillet of veal in eight equal medallions and flatten each piece between sheets of plastic wrap.

Sweat half the chopped onion in 1 Tbsp/15 g of the butter and half the oil until transparent. Leave to cool.

Add the sautéed onion, a sprinkling of herbs, the egg, half the cream and the Gruyère to the ground veal. Mix well and season with salt and pepper.

Spread a little of the mixture over each piece of veal. Fold in the sides and roll each piece neatly to make a *paupiette*. Wrap two pieces of bacon around each *paupiette* and secure with toothpicks.

Heat the remaining oil and 2 Tbsp/

14 oz/400 g fillet of veal
⅓ cup/40 g chopped onion
6 Tbsp/90 g unsalted butter
2 Tbsp/25 ml olive oil
freshly chopped herbs such as tarragon, parsley or chives
1 egg, beaten
½ cup less 1 Tbsp/100 ml heavy cream
4 tsp/20 g finely chopped Gruyère
1 cup/100 g finely ground veal
8 slices of bacon, cut in half
1 Tbsp/10 g chopped shallot
1½ cups/100 g button mushrooms
½ cup less 1 Tbsp/100 ml dry sherry
1 cup less 2 Tbsp/200 ml jus de veau (page 197)
1 clove of garlic, crushed
5 cups/750 g chopped plum tomato fillets
½ bay leaf
4 portions of Gnocchi alla Romana (page 186)
salt and freshly milled pepper
20 tiny sage leaves

Serves 4

25 g of the butter in a *sauteuse*. Season the *paupiettes* with salt and pepper, brown on all sides, then cook at 350°F/180°C for about 10 minutes until golden brown. Remove from the *sauteuse* and keep warm. Discard the fat.

Sweat the shallot in 2 Tbsp/25 g of the butter. Add to the mushrooms and sweat for a further 1 minute. Add the sherry and reduce by half. Add the jus de veau and remaining cream and reduce to the required consistency. Season to taste and stir in 1 Tbsp/15 g of the butter.

Sweat the remaining onion and garlic in the remaining butter. Add the tomato, bay leaf, salt and pepper. Simmer for about 10 minutes.

Arrange two *paupiettes* on each plate, and spoon a little sauce over each portion. Spoon a little tomato on each plate, top with a portion of Gnocchi alla Romana and garnish with sage leaves.

CANON D'AGNEAU POCHE, SAUCE RAIFORT

POACHED LAMB WITH HORSERADISH SAUCE

2 racks of lamb, each having 6–8 ribs
1½-inch/3.5-cm piece of medium carrot, cut in *brunoise*
2¼-inch/5.5-cm piece of leek, cut in *brunoise*
5½-inch/13.5-cm piece of celery, cut in *brunoise*
¼ cup/50 g unsalted butter
14 oz/400 g new potatoes, cut in ¼-inch/.5-cm cubes
4 cups/1 liter strong chicken stock (page 194)
¼ cup/50 ml dry white wine
1 cup less 2 Tbsp/200 ml heavy cream
freshly grated horseradish
4 Tbsp/10 g finely chopped parsley
salt and freshly milled pepper

Serves 4

Remove all the bones and fat from the racks of lamb.

Sweat the diced vegetables quickly in 2 Tbsp/25 g of the butter.

Place the potatoes in a saucepan of cold salted water and quickly bring to a boil. Drain and add to the diced vegetables. Add about half of the stock, to just cover. Season with salt and pepper. Simmer gently for about 10 minutes until tender.

Bring the remaining chicken stock to a boil, reduce to a simmer and add the lamb. Poach gently without boiling for 8 minutes until the lamb is pink.

Remove from the saucepan and keep warm.

Reduce the white wine, then add the chicken stock and reduce. Add the cream, freshly grated horseradish to taste and freshly chopped parsley. Season to taste and stir in the remaining butter.

Cut the lamb in ¼-inch/.5-cm thick slices and arrange some on each plate. Position some potatoes on each plate and pour a small amount of stock over the meat. Serve the horseradish sauce separately and pour on to the meat at the last minute.

TOURNEDOS DE BOEUF BACCHUS

FILET MIGNON WITH WILD MUSHROOMS

¼ cup/50 ml oil
5 Tbsp/75 g unsalted butter
4 × 5½ oz/165 g filet mignon
2 Tbsp/20 g chopped shallot
2½ oz/65 g prepared snails, cut in quarters
½ cup less 1 Tbsp/100 ml red wine
1 cup less 2 Tbsp/200 ml jus de veau (page 197)
2⅔ cups/100 g assorted wild mushrooms, cleaned
freshly chopped herbs such as tarragon and chervil
4 Pommes Savoyard (page 180)
salt and freshly milled pepper

Serves 4

Heat the oil and 2 Tbsp/25 g of the butter and fry the pieces of beef quickly on both sides to seal, then cook according to taste. Remove from the pan and keep warm.

Discard the fat, add 1 Tbsp/15 g of the butter and half the shallot. Sweat until transparent, then add the snails and red wine, then reduce. Add the jus de veau and reduce to the required consistency. Season to taste and stir in 1 Tbsp/15 g of the butter.

Place the remaining shallot and the remaining butter in a saucepan and sweat. Add the wild mushrooms and sweat for about 2 minutes. Season to taste and add the herbs.

Place a Pomme Savoyard on each plate and position a piece of beef on each one. Pour a little sauce over each portion and garnish with the wild mushrooms.

Serve with Légumes Variés Royal (page 188).

COTE DE VEAU NORMANDE

VEAL CUTLET NORMANDE

½ cup/100 g unsalted butter
4 × 9 oz/250 g lean veal cutlets
⅓ cup/40 g minced onion
24 white peppercorns, crushed
1¼ cups/300 ml hard cider
1 cup less 2 Tbsp/200 ml jus de veau (page 197)
½ cup less 1 Tbsp/100 ml heavy cream
2 cups/65 g button mushrooms
freshly chopped herbs
2 oz/50 g puff pastry dough (page 200)
1 eating apple, quartered
1 egg yolk, beaten
poppy seeds
sesame seeds
14 oz/400 g spinach leaves, blanched
grated nutmeg
salt and freshly milled pepper

Serves 4

Melt ¼ cup/50 g of the butter and fry the veal cutlets until just pink. Remove from the pan and discard the fat. Sweat the onions in 1 Tbsp/15 g of the butter until transparent. Add the peppercorns and cider and reduce by two-thirds. Add the jus de veau and cream, and reduce to the desired consistency. Season with salt and pepper and pass through fine cheesecloth.

Sweat the mushrooms in 1 Tbsp/15 g of the butter. Add the sauce to the mushrooms and stir in 1 Tbsp/15 g of the butter and a sprinkling of herbs.

Roll out the puff pastry dough and use to wrap each apple quarter. Brush with beaten egg yolk and cover with a sprinkling of poppy and sesame seeds. Leave to rest for 20 minutes, then bake at 400°F/200°C for about 15 minutes until golden brown.

Thoroughly dry the spinach and toss very quickly in the remaining butter. Season with a pinch of nutmeg and salt and pepper.

Place some spinach on each plate, arrange a veal cutlet on the top, spoon some sauce and mushrooms over and garnish with an apple fleuron.

ROSETTES DE BOEUF AU CERFEUIL

FILET MIGNON WITH CHERVIL

¼ lb/100 g small young carrots	
sugar	
4⅓ Tbsp/65 g unsalted butter	
¼ lb/100 g very small zucchini	
heaped 1 cup/200 g Cannoise (page 193)	
1½ lb/550 g filet mignon, cut in 8 pieces	
¼ cup/50 ml dry white wine	
½ cup less 1 Tbsp/100 ml jus de veau (page 197)	
½ cup less 1 Tbsp/100 ml heavy cream	
4 tsp/20 g Meaux mustard	
salt and freshly milled pepper	
20 sprigs of chervil	

Serves 4

Canalé the carrots and cut in ⅛-inch/ .3-cm thick slices. Place a generous pinch of sugar and 2 tsp/10 g of the butter in a saucepan and add a small amount of water. Cover and cook the carrots until tender.

Peel two of the zucchini, blanch the skin in boiling salted water, drain and refresh. *Canalé* the remaining zucchini, then blanch in boiling salted water. Refresh and cut in ⅛-inch/.3-cm thick slices. Melt 1 Tbsp/15 g of the butter and toss the zucchini slices very quickly. Season with salt and pepper.

Warm the Cannoise. Place a 3½–4-inch/9–10-cm metal ring on each plate. Half-fill with Cannoise and level the surface. Remove the rings. Arrange the sliced carrots and sliced zucchini decoratively on the top. Warm the zucchini skins and wrap around the Cannoise chartreuse.

Heat 2 Tbsp/25 g of the butter and fry the pieces of beef on both sides according to taste. Remove from the pan and discard the fat. *Déglacé* with the white wine, reduce and add the jus de veau and cream. Reduce to the desired consistency. Stir in the mustard, season to taste and stir in the remaining butter.

Pour a little sauce on each plate, arrange the beef on top and garnish with sprigs of chervil.

ESCALOPES DE ROGNONS
ET RIS DE VEAU AUX OIGNONS VERTS

KIDNEY AND SWEETBREAD WITH HORSE-RADISH AND SCALLION SAUCE

Cut the veal sweetbread in ½-inch/1-cm thick slices. Cut the veal kidneys in ½-inch/1-cm thick slices, leaving a very small amount of fat around each slice.

Place a small knob of butter and a generous pinch of sugar in a saucepan and caramelize lightly. Add the carrots and toss in this glaze. Add 2 Tbsp/25 ml of water or vegetable stock, salt and pepper, cover and cook until *al dente*.

Cook four of the scallions in boiling salted water until *al dente* and refresh. Cook the asparagus tips in boiling salted water until *al dente* and refresh. Cut the remaining scallions in very small dice.

Season the veal kidneys and veal sweetbread with salt and pepper, then dust lightly with flour. Heat the oil and

¾ lb/350 g veal sweetbreads, prepared
¾ lb/350 g veal kidneys
5 Tbsp/75 g unsalted butter
sugar
¼ lb/100 g young carrots
8 scallions
¼ lb/100 g asparagus tips
all-purpose flour
¼ cup/50 ml oil
¼ cup/50 ml dry white wine
¼ cup/50 ml chicken stock (page 194)
¼ cup/50 ml vegetable stock (page 206)
½ cup less 1 Tbsp/100 ml heavy cream
1⅓ Tbsp/20 g freshly grated horseradish
freshly chopped parsley
salt and freshly milled pepper

Serves 4

2 Tbsp/25 g of the butter. Fry the kidneys until pink and fry the sweetbread very quickly on both sides until golden brown. Remove from the pan and keep warm.

Discard the fat from the pan, add 2 tsp/10 g of the butter and sweat the finely chopped scallions. Add the white wine, chicken and vegetable stocks and reduce. Add the cream and reduce to the required consistency. Add the freshly grated horseradish to the sauce, season to taste and stir in 2 Tbsp/25 g of the butter. Stir in a little chopped parsley. Spoon a little sauce onto each plate.

Melt the remaining butter and toss all the vegetables. Season with salt and pepper. Arrange the sweetbread and kidneys alternately on the sauce. Garnish with the vegetables.

LES TROIS ROSETTES
SUR SPAGHETTI DE LEGUMES AU SAUCE DE CORIANDRE

MEDALLIONS OF VEAL, BEEF AND LAMB

Cut all the carrots and kohlrabi in "spaghetti", but only cut the outside skin of the zucchini in "spaghetti". Blanch in boiling salted water for about 1 minute, then refresh.

Cut the potatoes in cylindrical shapes, about 1½-inch/4-cm wide, then cut in wafer-thin slices. Dry on a dish towel and toss in hot oil until just tender but not colored. Drain and dry. Season with salt and pepper.

Reserve about one-fourth of the fresh cilantro for the sauce. Place one large cilantro leaf on a slice of potato and cover with another slice of potato. Press down well. Repeat until all the potato and cilantro leaves are used.

Heat the oil and 2 Tbsp/25 g of the butter and fry the medallions of meat

¼ lb/100 g carrots
¼ lb/100 g kohlrabi
¼ lb/100 g zucchini
1 lb 2 oz/500 g potatoes
oil for blanching
2 large sprigs fresh cilantro
¼ cup/50 ml oil
¾ cup/175 g unsalted butter
7 oz/200 g fillet of veal, trimmed and cut in 4 medallions
7 oz/200 g fillet of beef, trimmed and cut in 4 medallions
7 oz/200 g loin of lamb, trimmed and cut in 4 medallions
1 cup less 1 Tbsp/100 ml Noilly Prat
¼ cup/50 ml jus de veau (page 197)
1 cup less 2 Tbsp/200 ml heavy cream
salt and freshly milled pepper

Serves 4

on both sides according to taste. Remove from the pan and keep warm.

Discard the fat from the pan and *déglacé* with the Noilly Prat. Add the jus de veau and cream, and reduce to the required consistency.

Chop the reserved cilantro, add to the sauce, season with salt and pepper and stir in 1 Tbsp/15 g of the butter.

Melt 2½ Tbsp/40 g of the butter and toss the vegetable "spaghetti" until warm. Season and arrange some in the middle of each plate. Place the medallions of meat on top.

Fry the slices of potato very quickly in the remaining butter until they are crisp and golden, then drain on a dish towel. Arrange around the meat and pour a little sauce over each portion.

FOIE DE VEAU
AU CONFIT D'ECHALOTES ET MIEL

CALF'S LIVER WITH SHALLOTS

Peel the skin from the calf's liver and cut in thin slices. Season with salt and pepper and dust with the flour. Heat the oil and half the butter and fry the liver very quickly on both sides so it remains pink. Remove from the pan and keep warm.

Discard the fat remaining in the pan, *déglacé* with half the white wine and reduce. Add the jus de veau, season to taste and stir in half the remaining butter, the tomato diamonds and a

1¼ lb/600 g calf's liver
2½ Tbsp/20 g all-purpose flour
¼ cup/50 ml oil
½ cup/100 g unsalted butter
1 cup less 2 Tbsp/200 ml dry white wine
1¼ cups/300 ml jus de veau (page 197)
1½ Tbsp/25 g plum tomato diamonds
fresh thyme leaves
1½ cups/200 g chopped shallots
½ clove of garlic, crushed
¼ cup/50 ml herb-flavored white-wine vinegar
1 Tbsp/15 g honey
½ cup/20 g chopped fresh herbs such as chervil, basil and chives

Serves 4

sprinkling of fresh thyme leaves.

Sweat the shallots and garlic in the remaining butter until transparent and very soft. Add the vinegar and reduce. Add the remaining white wine and reduce. Add the honey and herbs, and season to taste.

Arrange a little of the shallot mixture in the center of each plate, place slices of calf's liver on top and pour the sauce around each portion.

MIGNONS DE VEAU AUX CEPES

MEDALLIONS OF VEAL WITH CEPS

½ cup / 100 g unsalted butter
¼ cup / 50 ml oil
8 × 3 oz / 75 g medallions of veal
1 Tbsp / 10 g chopped shallot
½ clove of garlic, crushed
2⅔ cups / 100 g cleaned and sliced fresh ceps
½ cup less 1 Tbsp / 100 ml dry white wine
1 cup less 2 Tbsp / 200 ml jus de veau (page 197)
¼ lb / 100 g assorted noodles (page 199)
freshly chopped mixed herbs such as chervil, chives and tarragon
salt and freshly milled pepper

Serves 4

Heat 2 Tbsp / 25 g of the butter and the oil, and fry the mignons of veal until pink. Remove from the pan and keep in a warm place. Discard the fat.

Sweat half the shallots in 2 Tbsp / 25 g of the butter until transparent. Add the garlic and sweat for a further minute. Add the ceps to the shallots and sweat for about 2 minutes. Season with salt and pepper and remove from the pan.

Add the remaining shallots to the pan and sweat with 1 Tbsp / 15 g of the butter. Add the white wine and reduce by two-thirds. Add the jus de veau and reduce to the required consistency. Season to taste and stir in 1 Tbsp / 15 g of the butter.

Cook the noodles in a large amount of boiling salted water with a dash of oil until *al dente*. Refresh, then drain and toss in the remaining butter. Season to taste.

Twist about a quarter of the noodles on a fork into a spiral on each plate, arrange the mignons on top, spoon a little sauce over each and garnish with ceps, sprinkled with herbs.

NOISETTES D'AGNEAU NICOISES

MEDALLIONS OF LAMB NICOISE		*Serves 4*

2 small green zucchini	
2 small yellow zucchini	
4 tiny zucchini with their flowers, blanched	
⅓ cup/65 g Cannoise (page 193)	
¼ cup/50 ml oil	
½ cup/100 g unsalted butter	
8 × 3 oz/75 g medallions of lamb (page 193)	
2 Tbsp/25 ml Madeira	
¼ cup/50 ml truffle juice (page 198)	
1¼ cups/300 ml jus de veau (page 197)	
1⅓ Tbsp/10 g chopped truffle	
¾ cup/150 g mushroom duxelle (page 199)	
1 clove of garlic, crushed	
1 plum tomato, cut in fillets	
¾ oz/20 g fresh foie gras, cut in 4 small rounds	
all-purpose flour	
4 slices of truffle	
salt and freshly milled pepper	

Canalé the zucchini evenly, then blanch in boiling salted water for about 2 minutes. Drain and refresh, then cut at an angle in slices about ⅛-inch/ .3-cm thick.

Dry the zucchini flowers on a dish towel and cut the zucchini in thin slices to fan out. Remove the stamens from inside the flowers and fill with the Cannoise. Place in a buttered heatproof dish, season and cover with plastic wrap. Steam for about 3 minutes.

Heat the oil and 2 Tbsp/25 g of the butter, and fry the medallions until pink, turning frequently. Remove from the pan and discard the fat. Add the Madeira and truffle juice, and reduce by half. Add the jus de veau and reduce to the required consistency. Pass through a fine strainer or cheesecloth. Season to taste, stir in 2 Tbsp/25 g of the butter and add the chopped truffle.

Arrange some hot mushroom duxelle in a neat circle on each plate.

Melt 2 Tbsp/25 g of the butter with the crushed garlic and toss the zucchini slices and tomato fillets until warm. Season to taste and arrange around the mushroom duxelle.

Place two medallions on each plate.

Season the foie gras and dust with flour. Fry very quickly on both sides in the remaining butter in a heavy-bottomed pan. Warm the slices of truffle in the sauce.

Spoon a little sauce over the medallions. Place the foie gras on top and garnish with the slices of truffle. Fan a zucchini flower carefully on each plate.

CANETON SOUFFLE
AU CHATELAIN DE TOURBILLON

THE SQUIRE OF TOURBILLON'S DUCK

Featured regularly on the Restaurant menu now, this dish exemplifies the spirit of freemasonry that exists between distinguished chefs. It was created by Virlogeux, maître-chef of the Grill in the glittering years between the world wars. He subsequently moved to another hotel where he gave the recipe to a young colleague, who in turn passed it back to Anton Edelmann years later!

Bone out the duck with a small knife (page 205). Reserve all the bones.

Sweat the shallots and garlic in the oil and 2 Tbsp/25 g of the butter until transparent. Add the mushrooms and sweat for 1–2 minutes. Add half the truffle juice. Reduce, then leave to cool. Add to the boned duck meat and pork, then grind coarsely.

Finely grind the pork fat with the bread crumbs and add to the meat mixture. Combine with the egg, egg yolk, heavy cream, chopped truffle and diced foie gras, and season generously. Use this mixture to fill the duck and reshape. Sew up all the

1 duck, dressed
4 Tbsp/40 g minced shallots
½ clove of garlic, crushed
¼ cup/50 ml oil
4⅓ Tbsp/65 g unsalted butter
1½ cups/100 g quartered mushrooms
½ cup less 1 Tbsp/100 ml truffle juice (page 198)
¼ lb/100 g boned duck thigh meat
7 oz/200 g loin of pork
¼ cup/50 g pork fat
1 cup/50 g fresh white bread crumbs, soaked in a little milk and squeezed
1 egg
1 egg yolk
¼ cup/50 ml heavy cream
1⅓ Tbsp/10 g chopped truffle
1 oz/25 g foie gras, diced
1 cup/100 g mirepoix (page 207)
2 large duck breasts
¼ cup/50 ml oz ruby port
1¼ cups/300 ml jus de veau (page 197)
½ cup/75 g grapes, skinned and pitted
½ cup/50 g walnut halves, blanched in milk and peeled
salt and freshly milled pepper
12–16 sprigs of chervil

Serves 6–8

openings with a trussing needle and fine string.

Melt half the remaining butter, brush the duck and season generously. Place in a roasting pan on the duck bones and mirepoix and roast at 350°F/180°C for about 1 hour, basting frequently. Add the duck breasts to the roasting pan and cook for a further 15 minutes. Remove from the oven and leave to rest in a warm place for at least 15 minutes.

Discard the fat from the roasting pan. Add the remaining truffle juice, port and jus de veau. Simmer for 15 minutes, skimming frequently. Season to taste and stir in the remaining butter. Pass through a fine strainer or cheesecloth.

Cut the duck in ½-inch/1-cm thick slices and place one in the center of each plate. Remove the skin from the duck breasts, cut in thin slices and arrange a few on each plate. Add the grapes and walnuts to the sauce and pour a little around each portion. Garnish with sprigs of chervil.

DELICE DE VOLAILLE
A LA HOMARDINE

CHICKEN BREAST WITH
LOBSTER FILLING

Remove the mignon fillet from each chicken breast and split by making a cut horizontally almost through each one. Open out and place all the pieces of chicken between sheets of plastic wrap and beat lightly to flatten (page 192). Season with salt and pepper.

Pass the raw lobster eggs through a fine strainer, add to the chicken mousse and mix well. Spread a little chicken mousse very thinly on each breast, leaving a ¼-inch/.5-cm border. Dry the spinach, season and lay on top of the chicken mousse. Spread another thin layer of chicken mousse on top.

Place half a lobster tail on each breast and top with the reserved chicken fillets. Fold the pointed end

4 × 4½ oz/120 g halved and boneless chicken breasts, trimmed
1 Tbsp/10 g raw lobster eggs
⅔ cup/75 g chicken mousse (page 206)
2½ oz/65 g young spinach leaves, blanched
2 × 1 lb/450 g hen lobsters, preferably Scottish, cooked for 5 minutes (page 207), shells removed
4⅓ Tbsp/65 g unsalted butter
1 cup/150 g vegetables baton-shaped such as carrots, zucchini, turnips and rutabaga, blanched
1 cup less 2 Tbsp/200 ml lobster sauce (page 198)
¼ cup/40 g wild rice, cooked
1 cup/65 g pilaf rice (page 200)
1 cup/65 g saffron rice (page 200)
4 Tbsp/10 g chopped fresh herbs such as chervil, tarragon and cilantro
salt and freshly milled pepper
dried lobster eggs (page 207), optional

Serves 4

and sides of the chicken breast over the lobster to form a neat parcel. Wrap each piece of chicken in plastic wrap and steam for about 8 minutes.

Melt 2⅔ Tbsp/40 g of the butter and sauté the vegetable batons, season to taste and arrange some on each plate.

Remove the plastic wrap from the chicken breasts, cut in slices and arrange on top of the vegetables. Warm the lobster claws and arrange on one side of the chicken. Pour a little sauce around each portion.

Mix the three rices with the herbs. Melt the remaining butter and toss the rice mixture until warm. Season to taste and arrange a little on each plate. Garnish with dried lobster eggs, if wished.

POULET SAUTE A LA ROMAINE

ROMAN-STYLE CHICKEN SAUTE

2 × 2½ lb / 1.25 kg chickens
1 Tbsp / 10 g all-purpose flour
¼ cup / 50 ml oil
5 Tbsp / 75 g unsalted butter
heaped ⅓ cup / 50 g minced onion
½ clove of garlic, crushed
⅔ cup / 100 g chopped plum tomato fillets
1¾ cups / 120 g button mushrooms, cut in quarters
1 red pepper, cut in small triangles
1 green pepper, cut in small triangles
½ cup less 1 Tbsp / 100 ml dry white wine
1¼ cups / 300 ml jus de veau (page 197)
1 sprig of sage, chopped
1 sprig of rosemary, chopped
salt and freshly milled pepper
7 oz / 200 g Polenta (page 186), cut in diamonds

Serves 4

Remove the legs and wings from each chicken. Cut the chickens in half. Cut off the knuckle from each chicken drumstick and scrape the tip of the bone clean. Remove the thighbone from each thigh. Make an incision in the center of each thigh and push the drumstick bone through the cut to form a neat shape (page 206). Trim each breast. Season all the pieces of chicken with salt and pepper, and dust with the flour. Heat half the oil and 2 Tbsp / 25 g of the butter and fry the chicken until golden brown. Remove from the pan and discard the fat.

Add the remaining oil and 2 Tbsp / 25 g of the butter to the pan and sweat the onion slowly until transparent.

Add the garlic, tomato and mushrooms and sweat for a further 2 minutes. Add the peppers and white wine, and reduce. Add the jus de veau, sage and rosemary.

Return the pieces of chicken to the pan, season with salt and pepper, cover and braise at 350°F / 180°C for about 20 minutes.

Remove the chicken and remove all the bones from each breast. Reduce the sauce to the required consistency. Season to taste and stir in the remaining butter.

Arrange some of the chicken in the center of each plate, spoon a little of the sauce on top and garnish with fried diamonds of Polenta.

SUPREME DE CANARD AUX RAISINS

DUCK BREAST WITH GRAPES IN A PUFF PASTRY LATTICE

2 × 4½ lb/2 kg ducks, dressed
scant ⅓ cup/40 g chicken mousse (page 206)
1½ oz/40 g fresh foie gras
¼ cup/50 g unsalted butter
¼ cup/50 ml oil
½ cup/50 g mirepoix (page 207)
½ cup less 1 Tbsp/100 ml dry white wine
2¼ cups/500 ml jus de veau (page 197)
4½ oz/120 g puff pastry dough (page 200)
1 egg yolk, beaten
⅓ cup/65 g green lentils, soaked in cold water for at least 4 hours
1 cup/65 g vegetables cut in *brunoise*, such as leek, celery and carrot
scant ⅔ cup/100 g carrot purée (page 193)
scant ⅔ cup/100 g celery root purée (page 193)
12 turned carrots (page 181), cooked in stock
12 turned turnips (page 181), cooked in stock
¼ cup/40 g snow peas, blanched
heaped 1½ cups/100 g white grapes, peeled and pits removed
salt and freshly milled pepper
4 sprigs of chervil

Serves 4

Remove the wishbone and legs from each duck and take off the breasts. Remove all the fat from the breasts, then make an incision with a long, narrow-bladed knife through the center of each breast, starting at the thick end and working right down to the pointed end to form a pocket. Fill each pocket with a small amount of chicken mousse. Cut the foie gras in batons and insert one in each breast.

Heat 1 Tbsp/15 g of the butter and half the oil. Season the duck breasts with salt and pepper and seal very quickly on both sides. Leave to cool.

Chop the duck carcasses and legs and place in a roasting pan with the remaining oil. Cook at 425°F/220°C for about 20 minutes or until brown. Add the mirepoix and cook for a further 10 minutes. Discard the fat, add the white wine and reduce. Add the jus de veau and simmer for about 20 minutes, skimming frequently. Remove the bones, then pass the sauce through a fine strainer, season to taste and stir in half the remaining butter.

Roll out the pastry dough about ⅛-inch/.3-cm thick and mark with a trellis cutter (page 200). Cut in four equal portions. Wrap each duck breast in a piece of lattice dough and brush with beaten egg yolk. Leave to rest for at least 20 minutes in a cool place.

Cook the lentils in boiling salted water for about 15 minutes. Drain thoroughly. Sweat the finely diced vegetables in the remaining butter until tender. Mix in the lentils and season with salt and pepper.

Bake the duck breasts at 425°F/220°C for 8 minutes or until golden.

Warm the carrot and celery root purées separately. Shape four quenelles with the carrot purée and place one on each plate; shape four quenelles with the celery root purée and place one on each plate. Arrange some of the turned carrots, turnips and snow peas on each plate. Place a little of the lentil mixture on each plate. Cut the duck breasts and arrange on top.

Add the grapes to the sauce, warm gently and pour some sauce around each duck breast. Garnish with the grapes and sprigs of chervil.

JAMBONETTE DE VOLAILLE FARCIE AUX ECREVISSES

STUFFED CHICKEN LEG WITH CRAYFISH

4 medium-sized chicken legs
1 Tbsp/10 g chopped shallot
4⅓ Tbsp/65 g unsalted butter
3½ cups/250 g minced button mushrooms
4 Tbsp/10 g chopped fresh herbs such as thyme, tarragon and chives
scant ⅓ cup/40 g chicken mousse (page 206)
24 live crayfish
4 cups/1 liter vegetable stock (page 206)
2 Tbsp/25 ml olive oil
scant ½ cup/40 g mirepoix (page 207)
½ clove of garlic
¼ cup/50 ml brandy
1⅓ Tbsp/20 g tomato paste
½ cup less 1 Tbsp/100 ml dry sherry
2¼ cups/500 ml chicken stock (page 194)
1 cup less 2 Tbsp/200 ml heavy cream
salt and freshly milled pepper
4 sprigs of chervil

Serves 4

Bone out each chicken leg by easing the flesh away from the bone starting at the thigh and working down to the drumstick, taking care not to pierce the skin.

Sweat the shallot in 2⅔ Tbsp/40 g of the butter until transparent. Add the mushrooms and cook very quickly. Season with salt and pepper and leave to cool.

Add the mushrooms and herbs to the chicken mousse and mix well.

Cook the crayfish in the boiling vegetable stock for 2 minutes. Drain and refresh. Remove and reserve the shells. Trim the crayfish and reserve twenty tails for garnish. Cut the remaining tails in half and mix with the trimmings into the prepared stuffing. Season generously and use to fill the chicken legs and sew up with a trussing needle and fine string.

Season the chicken legs with salt and pepper and roast at 375°F/190°C in 1 Tbsp/15 g of the butter and half the oil until golden brown and well cooked. Remove and keep warm. Discard the fat.

Chop the crayfish heads and shells very finely. Heat the remaining oil and fry the shells very quickly. Add the mirepoix and garlic and fry quickly, then flame with the brandy. Add the tomato paste, half the sherry and the chicken stock, and simmer for about 20 minutes, skimming frequently. Pass through a fine strainer or cheesecloth and reduce. Add the cream and reduce to the required consistency. Stir in the remaining sherry and butter. Season to taste.

Arrange a piece of chicken on each plate. Add the reserved crayfish to the sauce and heat gently. Spoon a little sauce over each portion.

Garnish with sprigs of chervil and serve with Crêpes aux Maïs et Poivrons (page 182).

GAME PIE

Improbable as it may sound, this popular dish was developed during the Second World War. Game was not rationed and the owners of many Scottish estates sold birds and venison to The Savoy. Obviously some of the other ingredients had to be omitted at that time. The addition of oxtail is an innovation that gives more strength to the sauce than the traditional drumstick.

Cut the game birds in half. Cut the venison in two large chunks. Season the meats with salt and pepper and dust lightly with the flour.

Heat half the oil and 2 Tbsp/25 g of the butter and fry all the meats until golden brown. Remove from the pan and discard the fat. Add the remaining oil and 1 Tbsp/15 g of the butter, then add the mirepoix and fry for about 5 minutes until lightly colored. Add the garlic and tomato paste and sweat for a further 2–3 minutes, stirring constantly. Add the red wine and reduce.

Add the jus de veau, herbs and peppercorns with the oxtail and tomato. Cover with a lid and braise at 325°F/170°C for about 1½ hours. Stir occasionally, adding a little extra stock if necessary. Add the game birds and venison and braise for a further 20 minutes, or until the meats are tender. Remove from the oven and remove all the meats from the sauce.

Place the oxtail in an oblong, deep baking dish or English pie dish. Remove all the bones from the game birds and divide the breast and legs.

1 grouse or pheasant, dressed
1 partridge, dressed
7 oz/200 g loin or haunch of venison
2½ Tbsp/20 g all-purpose flour
¼ cup/50 ml oil
5 Tbsp/75 g unsalted butter
½ cup/50 g mirepoix (page 207)
1 clove of garlic, crushed
1 Tbsp/20 g tomato paste
1 cup less 2 Tbsp/200 ml red wine
1¼ cups/300 ml jus de veau (page 197)
½ bay leaf
1 sprig of thyme
24 peppercorns, crushed
10 oz/300 g oxtail, cut in small pieces
1 Tbsp/20 g chopped plum tomato fillets
1¾ cups/200 g chestnuts
2½ tsp/10 g sugar
½ cup less 1 Tbsp/100 ml dry white wine
⅔ cup/50 g small button mushrooms
10 large/50 g dried apricot halves, soaked in cold water for at least 1 hour
⅓ cup/50 g pearl onions, blanched
2 oz/50 g bacon, cut in thin strips and blanched
5 oz/150 g puff pastry dough (page 200)
1 egg yolk, beaten
salt and freshly milled pepper

Serves 4

Add the venison and game birds to the pie dish.

Pass the sauce through a fine strainer or cheesecloth, season to taste and stir in 1 Tbsp/15 g of the butter.

Make a cross-shaped incision with a small knife in each chestnut and place on a baking sheet and roast at 450°F/230°C until the points of the cut curl up. Remove the skins.

Place 2 tsp/10 g of the butter in a saucepan with the sugar and caramelize lightly. Add the white wine and reduce. Add the chestnuts and stir well until glazed. Reduce all the cooking liquid, add a small amount of the sauce and reduce until the chestnuts are evenly coated.

Melt the remaining butter and sauté the mushrooms very quickly. Season with salt and pepper. Add the apricots, chestnuts, pearl onions, bacon strips and mushrooms to the sauce and pour the sauce on to the meats.

Roll out the pastry dough to about 1-inch/2.5-cm larger in diameter than the dish. Brush the edges of the dough with egg yolk and place egg-side down over the dish so that it overhangs. Garnish with the trimmings and crisscross the surface with the back of a knife. Leave to rest for 20 minutes in a cool place, then brush with egg yolk. Bake at 400°F/200°C for about 25 minutes until golden brown. Trim the excess dough from around the dish.

Serve with Navets à la Dauphinoise (page 182).

CAILLE FARCIE
A LA DAUPHINOISE

**STUFFED QUAIL WITH
DAUPHINE POTATOES**

4 quails, dressed
3 oz/75 g stuffing for quail (page 201)
¼ cup/50 ml oil
scant ½ cup/40 g mirepoix (page 207)
1 cup less 2 Tbsp/200 ml dry white wine
1¼ cups/300 ml jus de veau (page 197)
12 peppercorns, crushed
4⅓ Tbsp/65 g unsalted butter
1 clove of garlic, halved
1⅛ lb/500 g new potatoes, cut in ⅛-inch/.3-cm slices
grated nutmeg
½ cup/50 g grated Gruyère
1¼ cups/300 ml heavy cream
2½ tsp/10 g superfine sugar
½ cup/75 g pearl onions
5 sprigs of rosemary
salt and freshly milled pepper

Serves 4

Cut each quail along the backbone and bone out each bird very carefully without perforating the skin (see boning a duck, page 205). Season the inside with salt and pepper. Use a little of the stuffing to fill each quail, then reshape and sew back to the original shape with a trussing needle and string.

Chop up the bones and roast with the oil at 425°F/220°C for about 10 minutes. Add the mirepoix and roast for a further 10 minutes. Discard the fat. Add half the white wine, the jus de veau and peppercorns to the roasting pan and simmer for about 20 minutes, skimming frequently. Pass through a fine strainer, reduce to the required consistency and season to taste. Stir in 2 Tbsp/25 g of the butter.

Butter a shallow ovenproof dish and rub the inside with the garlic, then layer the slices of potato, seasoning with nutmeg, salt and pepper, and sprinkling with Gruyère. Continue until the dish is full and finish with a layer of Gruyère. Bring the cream to a boil, season with salt and pepper and pour over the potatoes. Bake at 350°F/180°C for about 45 minutes, until tender. Keep warm.

Season the quails and roast at 425°F/220°C for about 20 minutes, basting frequently. Leave to rest for about 10 minutes.

Heat 2 Tbsp/25 g of the butter and the sugar in a saucepan and caramelize. Add the pearl onions and the remaining white wine and simmer until all the liquid has evaporated. Add a small amount of the sauce and reduce until the onions are tender and evenly glazed. Add the leaves from one sprig of rosemary.

Remove the strings from the quails. Arrange some potatoes on each plate, position a quail on one side with some pearl onions and pour some sauce over each portion. Fry the remaining sprigs of rosemary in the remaining butter and use to garnish each plate.

CANON DE CHEVREUIL FARCI AUX ABRICOTS

LOIN OF VENISON WITH APRICOT FILLING

Marinate the venison in 1 cup less 2 Tbsp/200 ml of the red wine with the mirepoix, peppercorns, bay leaf, thyme and juniper berry for two days. Remove from the marinade and strain the marinade, reserving the mirepoix and wine for the sauce.

Drain and dice the apricots. Sweat about one-third of the shallot in 1 Tbsp/15 g of the butter until transparent. Add the apricots, bread crumbs and half the herbs. Season with salt and pepper. Make a cavity through the center of each portion of venison using a sharpening steel and fill with the apricot stuffing.

Sweat the onions in half the oil and 2 Tbsp/25 g of the butter until transparent. Add the red-wine vinegar and remaining wine, and reduce. Add the Grenadine and reduce until the liquid has completely evaporated and the onions are very soft. Spoon into four timbale molds or egg cups.

Season the portions of venison with salt and pepper. Heat the remaining oil

4 × 5½ oz/165 g portions of loin of venison, trimmed
1 cup plus 2 Tbsp/275 ml red wine
scant ½ cup/40 g mirepoix (page 207)
24 peppercorns, crushed
½ bay leaf
1 sprig of thyme
1 juniper berry
1¾ cups/225 g dried apricots, soaked in cold water for at least 1 hour
2 Tbsp/20 g minced shallots
8 Tbsp/120 g unsalted butter
1 cup/50 g fresh white bread crumbs, sieved
4 Tbsp/10 g freshly chopped herbs
scant 3 cups/500 g minced onions
¼ cup/50 ml oil
2 Tbsp/25 ml red-wine vinegar
1 cup less 2 Tbsp/200 ml Grenadine
1 cup less 2 Tbsp/200 ml game stock (page 196)
½ cup less 1 Tbsp/100 ml jus de veau (page 197)
½ cup less 1 Tbsp/100 ml heavy cream
1½ cups/100 g chanterelles, cleaned
salt and freshly milled pepper
4 sprigs of mint

Serves 4

and 2 Tbsp/25 g of the butter and seal the meat on all sides. Roast at 425°F/220°C for 6–7 minutes. Remove from the pan, discard the fat, add the mirepoix and sweat in 1 Tbsp/15 g of the butter. Add the marinade and reduce by two-thirds. Add the game stock and jus de veau, and reduce to the required consistency. Add the cream, reduce and stir in 1 Tbsp/15 g of the butter. Season to taste, pass through a fine strainer or cheesecloth and add the remaining herbs.

Sweat the remaining shallot in the remaining butter. Add the chanterelles and sweat for a further 2 minutes. Season with salt and pepper.

Unmold the onion timbales and position one on each plate. Add the chanterelles to the sauce and pour a little on each plate. Cut each portion of venison in ½-inch/1-cm thick slices and arrange on top of the sauce. Garnish each onion timbale with a sprig of mint.

Serve with Spetzli (page 184).

DELICE DE ROUGE D'ECOSSE GASTRONOME

GROUSE WITH SAVOY CABBAGE

2 grouse, dressed
heaped ⅓ cup/65 g chicken mousse (page 206)
2 leeks, cooked
¼ cup/50 ml oil
½ cup/50 g mirepoix (page 207)
1 clove of garlic, crushed
1 sprig of thyme
1 bay leaf
12 peppercorns, crushed
½ cup less 1 Tbsp/100 ml red wine
1 cup less 2 Tbsp/200 ml jus de veau (page 197)
1 Tbsp/10 g chopped shallot
¼ cup/50 g unsalted butter
1 cup/75 g assorted wild mushrooms, cleaned
freshly chopped parsley
7 oz/200 g Chou Frisé à la crème (page 180)
salt and freshly milled pepper
4 heart-shaped croutons (page 195)

Serves 4

Remove the legs and wishbones from the grouse and reserve. Remove the breasts, trim and remove the fillets. Split by making a cut horizontally almost through each one. Open out and place all the pieces of grouse between sheets of plastic wrap and beat lightly to flatten (see chicken breasts, page 192). Season with salt and pepper. Spread some of the chicken mousse about ⅛-inch/.3-cm thick on to each breast, leaving a ¼-inch/.5-cm border.

Dry the leeks on a dish towel and cut in 1½-inch/4-cm lengths. Place some in the center of each grouse breast. Top each one with the reserved fillet and fold the pointed end and the sides over the leek to form a neat package. Wrap in plastic wrap and steam for about 8 minutes until pink.

Chop the grouse legs and carcasses. Roast with the oil at 425°F/220°C for about 10 minutes. Add the mirepoix, garlic, thyme, bay leaf and peppercorns, and roast for a further 10 minutes. Discard the fat and add the red wine. Reduce, add the jus de veau and simmer for about 20 minutes, skimming frequently. Pass through a fine strainer, reduce to the required consistency, season to taste and stir in 2 Tbsp/25 g of the butter.

Sweat the shallot in 2 Tbsp/25 g of the butter until transparent, add the wild mushrooms, season to taste and add a sprinkling of chopped parsley.

Arrange some of the cabbage on each plate. Remove the plastic wrap from the grouse and cut each one at an angle in four even slices. Place the slices of grouse on top of the cabbage. Spoon a little sauce over the slices of grouse and garnish with the wild mushrooms and heart-shaped croutons, dipped in chopped parsley.

DELICE DE PIGEONNEAU FARCI PERIGUEUX

STUFFED PIGEONS

Remove the wishbone and legs from each pigeon, carefully remove the breasts and chop up the bones and legs. Trim the breasts and make an incision with a long, narrow-bladed knife through the center of each breast, starting at the thick end and working right down to the pointed end, to form a pocket.

Cut the foie gras in four batons, season with salt and pepper and insert one in each breast. Wrap each breast carefully in caul.

Roast the pigeon bones in half the oil at 425°F/220°C for about 20 minutes or until brown, then add the mirepoix and cook for a further 10 minutes.

Discard the fat. Add the Madeira, truffle juice and jus de veau. Simmer for about 20 minutes, skimming frequently. Pass through fine cheesecloth, then reduce to the desired consistency and add the chopped truffle.

4 pigeons, dressed
1½ oz/40 g fresh foie gras
2½ oz/65 g caul (available from specialist butchers)
2 Tbsp/25 ml oil
½ cup/50 g mirepoix (page 207)
½ cup less 1 Tbsp/100 ml Madeira
½ cup less 1 Tbsp/100 ml truffle juice (page 198)
1 cup less 2 Tbsp/200 ml jus de veau (page 197)
1⅓ Tbsp/10 g chopped truffle
5 oz/150 g kohlrabi
14 oz/400 g zucchini
1¼ cups/300 ml heavy cream
⅔ cup/65 g grated Gruyère
2⅔ Tbsp/40 g unsalted butter
salt and freshly milled pepper

Serves 4

Cut the kohlrabi and zucchini in batons about 1½-inches/4-cm long, discarding the seeds from the zucchini. Cook the vegetables separately in boiling salted water until just tender and refresh.

Reduce the cream, add the kohlrabi and zucchini, season with salt and pepper and add the Gruyère at the last moment.

Heat half the butter and the remaining oil and fry the pigeon breasts very quickly for about 2 minutes on each side until pink, then remove from the pan. Discard the fat in the pan and add the sauce.

Arrange some of the kohlrabi and zucchini mixture on each of four plates and glaze under a hot broiler. Lay two pigeon breasts on top of each portion. Stir the remaining butter into the sauce and season to taste. Spoon a little sauce over the pigeon breasts.

SUPREME DE FAISAN POMPADOUR

PHEASANT POMPADOUR

Remove the legs, wishbones, skin and wings from the pheasants. Bone out the thighs and use the meat to prepare pheasant mousse (see below). Remove the breasts from the carcasses, and remove and reserve the fillets from each breast. Spread a little of the pheasant mousse on each breast and replace the fillet.

Chop the carcasses and roast with half the oil at 425°F/220°C for 10–15 minutes. Add the mirepoix and roast for a further 5 minutes.

Add the white wine, game stock, jus de veau, crushed peppercorns, bay leaf and sprig of thyme. Simmer for about 10 minutes, skimming frequently. Pass through a fine strainer or cheesecloth.

Fry the breasts of pheasant in the remaining oil and half the butter until pink. Remove the breasts and keep in a warm place.

2 pheasants, dressed
scant 2 cups/200 g pheasant mousse (see below)
¼ cup/50 ml oil
scant ½ cup/40 g mirepoix (page 207)
½ cup less 1 Tbsp/100 ml dry white wine
½ cup less 1 Tbsp/100 ml game stock (page 196)
1 cup less 2 Tbsp/200 ml jus de veau (page 197)
12 peppercorns, crushed
½ bay leaf
1 sprig of thyme
¼ cup/50 g unsalted butter
½ cup less 1 Tbsp/100 ml brown ale
1 tsp/5 ml cumin seeds
4 Rösti de Panais et Carottes (page 188)
1½ cups/200 g rutabaga, turned in long cylindrical shapes, cooked *al dente*
1¼ cups/200 g kohlrabi, turned in long cylindrical shapes, cooked *al dente*
1¼ cups/200 g carrots, turned in long cylindrical shapes, cooked *al dente*
¼ lb/100 g small Brussels sprouts, cooked *al dente*
3 oz/75 g bacon, cut in thin strips and blanched
freshly chopped parsley
salt and freshly milled pepper

Serves 4

Discard the fat, add the brown ale and reduce almost completely. Add the sauce and reduce to the required consistency. Mix the cumin seeds with a small amount of the remaining butter and mince. Add to the sauce and simmer for about 5 minutes.

Place a Rösti de Panais et Carottes on each plate. Arrange a breast of pheasant on top and pour a little sauce over each portion.

Melt the remaining butter and toss the bacon strips until crisp, then toss all the vegetables quickly. Sprinkle with chopped parsley, season with salt and pepper, and use to garnish the pheasant.

PHEASANT MOUSSE: Use the meat from the pheasant thighs; follow the recipe for chicken mousse (page 206).

PERDREAU MAURICE
BRAISE AUX MARRONS

MAURICE'S PARTRIDGE BRAISED WITH CHESTNUTS	*Serves 4*

4 partridges, dressed
2 Tbsp/25 ml oil
5 Tbsp/75 g unsalted butter
scant ½ cup/40 g mirepoix (page 207)
½ cup less 1 Tbsp/100 ml ruby port
1 cup less 2 Tbsp/200 ml game stock (page 196)
1 cup less 2 Tbsp/200 ml jus de veau (page 197)
24 peppercorns, crushed
1 sprig of thyme
½ bay leaf
2½ tsp/10 g superfine sugar
½ cup less 1 Tbsp/100 ml dry white wine
1¼ cups/150 g chestnuts
1⅓ cups/200 g Chou Frisé à la crème (page 180)
1⅓ cups/200 g Chou Rouge Braisé (page 184)
salt and freshly milled pepper

Cut each partridge in half and season with salt and pepper.

Heat the oil and 2 Tbsp/25 g of the butter and fry the partridges until brown on all sides. Remove from the pan and discard the fat.

Add 2 Tbsp/25 g of the butter to the pan and sweat the mirepoix. Add the port and reduce. Add the game stock, jus de veau, peppercorns, thyme and bay leaf.

Place the partridges in an ovenproof dish, add the sauce, cover and braise at 350°F/180°C for 12–15 minutes. Remove the partridges and remove the breastbones.

Pass the sauce through a fine strainer or cheesecloth. Bring to a boil, skim any fat from the surface, season and stir in half the remaining butter.

Place the remaining butter and the sugar in a saucepan and caramelize. Pour in the white wine and reduce.

Make a cross-shaped incision with a small knife in each chestnut, place on a baking sheet and roast at 450°F/230°C until the cut points curl up. Remove the skins.

Place the chestnuts in the wine reduction and reduce until the liquid has evaporated, then add about ¼ cup/50 ml of the sauce. Reduce until all the chestnuts are evenly coated and the sauce becomes a thick syrup.

Place a small amount of the green and red cabbage on each plate. Place half a partridge on each portion of cabbage. Garnish with chestnuts and spoon some sauce over each portion.

LES
DESSERTS

GATEAU DE CYGNES
A LA SAVOY

SAVOY SWAN GATEAU

Even in the annals of The Savoy, no party can rival the spectacular Gondola Dinner given by the American millionaire George A Kessler in July 1905 to celebrate his birthday. The guests dined in an enormous gondola floating in the old courtyard which had been flooded to a depth of several feet. Caruso sang arias as this gâteau was served.

5 oz/150 g choux pastry dough (page 194)

2⅓ Tbsp/25 g superfine sugar

3 cups/750 ml heavy cream

confectioners' sugar

1 round Genoese sponge, 8-inches/20-cm in diameter (page 197)

2⅔ Tbsp/40 ml kirsch

2⅔ Tbsp/40 ml sugar syrup (page 204)

¼ lb/100 g raspberries

generous ⅓ cup/50 g chopped blanched almonds, roasted

2 oz/50 g semisweet couverture chocolate, tempered (page 204)

Serves 10

Using a ½-inch/1-cm plain tip, pipe ten 1-inch/2.5-cm circles of choux pastry dough onto a buttered baking sheet. Bake at 400°F/200°C for 15 minutes.

Using a ⅛-inch/.3-cm plain tip, pipe ten "S" shapes in choux pastry dough onto a buttered baking sheet. Bake at 350°F/180°C for 10 minutes until crisp and golden.

Split the buns horizontally and then cut the tops in half.

Add the superfine sugar to the cream and whip until just firm.

To assemble the swans, use a small star tip to fill the bottoms of the choux buns with some of the cream. Place the top halves at an angle to give the impression of wings. Place an "S"-shaped piece of choux pastry in front of each bun for the neck. Dust each swan with confectioners' sugar.

Slice the Genoese sponge horizontally into three equal layers and moisten each with a little kirsch and sugar syrup. Place the first layer on a cake board or plate. Spread with some of the remaining cream and sprinkle with a few raspberries. Repeat with the next layer and top with the third layer of sponge.

Spread the top and sides of the sponge carefully with the remaining cream and run a comb scraper around the sides to give a decorative effect. Press the chopped almonds on to the sides of the gâteau.

Pour the chocolate on to a plate and leave to set. Pull a metal spoon over the surface of the chocolate to form curls. Arrange these in the center of the gâteau. Position the swans with the heads pointing inward.

BRULEE D'ORANGE
ET SA JULIENNE

BURNED ORANGE CREAM

1½ cups/350 ml heavy cream
4 egg yolks
¼ cup/50 g superfine sugar
1 vanilla bean
scant ⅔ cup/100 g orange segments (page 203)
2 Tbsp/20 g caramelized orange *julienne* (page 193)
2⅔ Tbsp/40 ml Grand Marnier
¼ cup/25 g sifted confectioners' sugar

Serves 4

Mix the cream, egg yolks and super-fine sugar together and pass through a fine strainer. Remove the seeds from the vanilla bean and stir into the cream mixture.

Divide the orange segments between four ramekins and scatter the caramelized orange *julienne* on top.

Add the Grand Marnier and divide the cream mixture between the ramekins. Cook at 300°F/150°C in a water bath for about 40 minutes until lightly set. Leave to cool.

Dust with the confectioners' sugar and glaze under a hot broiler to give a golden brown caramelized top.

JALOUSIE AUX FRUITS EN SAISON ET DEUX COULIS

FRUIT JALOUSIE

Roll out the puff pastry dough about ⅛-inch/.3-cm thick and cut two 20 × 4-inch/50 × 10-cm strips. Place one strip on a buttered baking sheet. Using a ½-inch/1-cm plain tip, pipe two lines of frangipane down the center of this strip. Mark the second strip with a trellis cutter.

Arrange the apricots and cherries alternately on top of the frangipane.

9 oz/250 g puff pastry dough (page 200)

4½ oz/120 g frangipane (page 196)

10 large apricot halves, poached and well drained

¼ cup/50 g Griottine cherries, well drained

1 egg yolk, beaten

apricot jam, sieved and warmed

confectioners' sugar

Serves 10

Brush the edges with egg yolk and carefully position the lattice strip on top. Seal the edges well, brush the surface of the dough with egg yolk and bake at 400°F/200°C for about 20 minutes until crisp and golden brown.

Brush carefully with apricot jam glaze and dust the edges with confectioners' sugar. Serve with strawberry and vanilla sauces (pages 201 and 205).

DEMI-MANGUE
ET SA GLACE DIANA

MANGO FILLED WITH ICE CREAM

2 medium-sized, ripe mangoes
1¾ cups/400 ml vanilla ice cream mixture (page 205)
¼ cup/50 ml raspberry sauce (page 201)
¼ cup/50 ml mango sauce (page 198)
12 raspberries
24 wild strawberries
4 sprigs of mint

Serves 4

Cut the mangoes in half lengthwise, removing the seeds carefully with a spoon. Scoop out most of the flesh and chill the skins.

Purée the mango in a blender or food processor and pass through a fine strainer. Add the mango purée to the vanilla ice cream mixture and freeze to a piping consistency.

Using a small wax paper piping bag, pipe a ring of raspberry sauce around the edge of each plate. Pipe an inner ring of mango sauce. Bring the two rings together with a toothpick to give a feathered design.

Using a large star tip pipe the mango ice cream into the chilled mango skins and position one in the center of each plate. Decorate the top of each with three raspberries, six wild strawberries and a sprig of mint. Serve with palmiers (page 200).

TERRINE DE FRUITS D'ETE

TERRINE OF SUMMER FRUITS	8 leaves of gelatin, soaked in cold water	*Serves 10*
	3 cups/750 ml sugar syrup (page 204)	
	2⅔ Tbsp/40 ml kirsch	
	¼ lb/100 g wild strawberries	
	¼ lb/100 g blueberries	
	¼ lb/100 g raspberries	
	¼ lb/100 g tayberries	
	scant 2 cups/450 ml lime sauce (page 197)	

Drain the excess water from the gelatin, then dissolve over a low heat in the sugar syrup. Leave to cool, then stir in the kirsch.

Arrange a layer of wild strawberries in the base of a 5-cup/1.25-liter terrine. Pour on sufficient syrup to just cover, then chill until set. Repeat the layering until all the fruit and syrup have been used, leaving each layer to set before adding the next. Chill the terrine until completely firm.

Cut the terrine in slices and position a slice on each plate. Pour a little lime sauce around each portion.

Other summer fruits may also be used, if desired.

PETIT GATEAU DE
REINETTE A MA FACON

APPLE CAKE WITH
ORANGE SABAYON SAUCE

Use half the butter to coat the inside of four individual ramekins (about 3½-inches/9-cm diameter and 1½-inches/4-cm high). Roll out the sweet pastry dough ⅛-inch/.3-cm thick and use to line the ramekins. Fill the ramekins with the apple slices.

Beat the sour cream with 2 Tbsp/25 g of the superfine sugar, half the flour and the egg. Pass through a fine strainer and flavor with vanilla. Cover the apples with this mixture. Bake at 375°F/190°C for 10 minutes.

Combine the chopped walnuts, remaining flour, brown sugar, a little

¼ cup/50 g unsalted butter
6 oz/175 g sweet pastry dough (page 204)
2 small Reinette apples, peeled, cored and thinly sliced
1 cup less 2 Tbsp/200 ml sour cream
scant ½ cup/90 g superfine sugar
7 Tbsp/65 g all-purpose flour
1 egg
a few drops of vanilla
3 Tbsp/25 g chopped walnuts
2⅓ Tbsp/25 g brown sugar
ground cinnamon
salt
confectioners' sugar
¼ cup/50 ml orange juice
¼ cup/50 ml lemon juice
4 egg yolks
1¼ cups/300 ml Marsala

Serves 4

cinnamon and a pinch of salt. Melt the remaining butter and mix with the dry ingredients to form a crumb texture. Sprinkle a little on top of each ramekin and bake for a further 10 minutes.

Leave to cool slightly, then turn out onto individual warm plates and dust with confectioners' sugar.

Beat the orange and lemon juices, egg yolks, remaining superfine sugar and Marsala over boiling water until the sauce becomes light and fluffy. Pour the sauce around each portion. Serve raspberry sauce (page 201) separately.

PECHE A LA MELBA EN CAGE

PEACH MELBA

2 large peaches
2½ cups/600 ml sugar syrup (page 204)
2¼ cups/250 g superfine sugar
½ cup less 1 Tbsp/100 ml water
2 tsp/10 g glucose
1¼ cups/300 ml raspberry sauce (page 201)
4 tulip baskets (page 172)
1¾ cups/400 ml vanilla ice cream (page 205)

Serves 4

Poach the peaches in the sugar syrup for 1 minute until the skin comes off easily. Peel, leave to cool, then cut in half and remove the stones.

Mix the sugar, water and glucose together in a small saucepan and place over a high heat. Brush the sides of the pan quite frequently with a little water to prevent any crystallization. Cook the sugar to the hard-crack stage (310°F/152°C on a candy thermometer). Leave to cool until the syrup becomes thick.

Oil the outside of a 4-inch/10-cm wide ladle. Dip two dessert forks in the sugar syrup and flick very fine threads over the upturned ladle, changing the direction of the threads to form a lattice effect. Turn the ladle on its side and finish with a thin line of sugar syrup around the edge of the ladle to form the bottom of the cage. As soon as it is cool, carefully remove the cage from the ladle and keep in a cool, dry place. Make three more cages in the same way.

Pour a little of the raspberry sauce on to each of four plates. Place a tulip basket in the center of each plate. Scoop a quarter of the vanilla ice cream in the center and set a peach half on top. Spoon over a little raspberry sauce. Carefully arrange a sugar cage on top of each tulip basket.

PETIT GATEAU DE FROMAGE CHAUD AU COULIS AUX FRUITS

WARM CHEESECAKE WITH FRUIT SAUCES		*Serves 4*

WARM CHEESECAKE WITH FRUIT SAUCES

Roll out the sweet pastry dough ⅛-inch/.3-cm thick and use to line four buttered ramekins.

Mix the soft cheese and superfine sugar together. Add the vanilla, salt, cornstarch, egg yolks, cream, lemon peel and lemon juice, and stir to a smooth consistency. Beat the egg white to a stiff peak and fold into the soft cheese mixture. Use this to fill the prepared ramekins and bake at 350°F/

6 oz/175 g sweet pastry dough (page 204)

½ cup/120 g low-fat cream cheese

¼ cup/50 g superfine sugar

few drops of vanilla

pinch of salt

heaped 1 Tbsp/10 g cornstarch

2 egg yolks

½ cup less 1 Tbsp/100 ml heavy cream

grated peel of 1 lemon

juice of ½ lemon

1 egg white

confectioners' sugar

½ cup less 1 Tbsp/100 ml of both mango and strawberry sauces (pages 198 and 201)

4 strawberries, chopped

scant ½ cup/75 g diced mango

Serves 4

180°C for 30–35 minutes until lightly set and golden brown. Leave to cool slightly, then turn out and dust with confectioners' sugar.

Swirl a quarter of the mango sauce in a spiral design on to each plate. Fill the remaining space with the strawberry sauce. Position a small cheesecake in the center of each plate and sprinkle the sauces with the chopped strawberries and diced mango.

FONDANT DE CHOCOLAT,
SAUCE DE NOISETTES AU COINTREAU

CHILLED CHOCOLATE FONDANT

Warm the vanilla sauce and stir in the filberts. Leave to stand for 1 hour and then pass through a fine strainer. Add the Cointreau.

Line the bottom and sides of a 5-cup/1.25-liter terrine neatly with very thin slices of the vanilla sponge.

Whisk the egg yolks and sugar over hot water until thick and pale. Stir in the brandy and 5 oz/150 g of the chocolate. Pass the chocolate mixture through a fine strainer and keep warm. Gently fold in the cream and

2 cups less 2 Tbsp/450 ml vanilla sauce (page 205)
heaped ½ cup/75 g filberts, roasted, skinned and ground
¼ cup/50 ml Cointreau
1 vanilla sponge sheet (page 205)
5 egg yolks
¼ cup/50 g superfine sugar
¼ cup/50 ml brandy
6 oz/175 g semisweet couverture chocolate, tempered (page 204)
2½ cups/600 ml heavy cream, lightly whipped
caramelized orange *julienne* (page 193)
10 fresh mint leaves

Serves 10

pour into the prepared terrine.

Freeze for about 2 hours or until firm but not frozen. Carefully turn out the fondant and cut in ¾-inch/2-cm thick slices.

Divide the filbert sauce between ten plates. Place a slice of the chocolate fondant in the centers and decorate each slice with a little caramelized orange *julienne* and a mint leaf. Pipe the remaining chocolate around the filbert sauce and feather it, using a toothpick.

PETIT PARFAIT
DE NOËL

CHRISTMAS PARFAIT

2 egg yolks	
¼ cup/50 g superfine sugar	
2 Tbsp/25 ml Crème de Menthe	
1¾ cups/400 ml heavy cream	
1 oz/25 g semisweet couverture chocolate, tempered (page 204)	
1 oz/25 g white couverture chocolate, tempered	
½ cup less 1 Tbsp/100 ml chocolate sauce (page 194)	
⅔ cup/150 ml orange sauce (page 200)	
1¾ cups/400 g Griottine cherries in brandy	
1 Tbsp/10 ml arrowroot	
4 sprigs of mint	

Serves 4

Beat the egg yolks, half the sugar and the Crème de Menthe over boiling water to form a light, fluffy sabayon. Leave to cool and pass through a fine strainer.

Reserve ⅔ cup/150 ml of the cream. Lightly whip the remainder and fold into the cold sabayon. Spoon this mixture into a half-circle sleeve mold lined with plastic wrap. Level the surface with a spatula, cover with plastic wrap and freeze for about 4 hours or until firm.

Unmold the parfait. Whip the reserved cream and spread evenly over the parfait. Pull a comb scraper across the cream to give a lined effect. Freeze for a further 30 minutes.

Fill a small wax paper piping bag with the plain chocolate and pipe four small Christmas tree outlines onto baking parchment. Before the chocolate sets, fill the center of each tree with a little of the white chocolate, making it run into the outline. Leave to set. Pipe four gates in plain chocolate on to baking parchment. Leave to set.

Pipe three loops of plain chocolate on to each plate. Leave to set. Then fill the outlined design with chocolate sauce. Pipe white chocolate into the center of each loop and feather it with a toothpick.

Mix the arrowroot with a little cherry juice. Heat the cherries in brandy, add the arrowroot mixture and cook over a low heat until slightly thickened.

Pour a little orange sauce around the edge of each plate and decorate with some of the cherries.

Cut the parfait in neat portions with a sharp, warm knife and arrange a slice at the top of the design. Position the chocolate designs on the top and decorate with the sprigs of mint. Serve the remaining hot cherries separately in a sauce boat.

PETITE BOMBE GLACÉE PAQUITA

ICED BOMBE PAQUITA

3 egg yolks
2⅔ Tbsp/40 ml Anisette
1¼ cups/250 g superfine sugar
1 cup less 2 Tbsp/200 ml heavy cream
3½ Tbsp/25 g filberts, roasted, skinned and finely chopped
thin slice vanilla sponge (page 205)
2 Tbsp/25 ml kirsch
4 egg whites
scant ¼ cup/50 g orange segments
2 oz/50 g pawpaw, turned
1 kiwi, turned

Serves 4

Beat the egg yolks, Anisette and 3½ Tbsp/40 g of the sugar over boiling water to form a light, fluffy sabayon. Pass through a fine strainer and leave to cool. Lightly whip the cream and fold in the filberts and sabayon. Spoon this mixture into four molds (about 2-inches/5-cm wide and 3-inches/7.5-cm high). Cover with plastic wrap and freeze until firm.

Cut the vanilla sponge into four 2-inch/5-cm circles and moisten with the kirsch. Dip the molds into hot water and unmold the *parfaits* on to the sponge circles. Position on chilled plates and place in the freezer.

Whisk the egg whites until stiff, then beat in the remaining sugar, a spoonful at a time until the mixture is thick and glossy. Using a small star tip, pipe the meringue up the sides of each parfait to cover completely. Glaze evenly under a hot broiler until light golden brown.

Arrange the fruit on the plate. Serve with raspberry sauce (page 201).

POIRE
SOUS SA CROUTE

PEAR IN PASTRY LATTICE

2 fresh pears, peeled and cored
2¼ cups/500 ml sugar syrup (page 204)
½ lb/225 g puff pastry dough (page 200)
3 oz/75 g frangipane (page 196)
1 egg yolk, beaten
¼ cup/25 g sifted confectioners' sugar
¼ cup/50 ml Poire William
1¼ cups/300 ml vanilla sauce (page 205)

Serves 4

Poach the pears gently in the sugar syrup. Leave to cool, then cut in half.

Roll out half the puff pastry dough about ⅛-inch/.3-cm thick and cut out four pear shapes slightly larger than the poached pear halves. Place the dough shapes on a buttered baking sheet and pipe a little frangipane in the center of each. Position the poached pear halves on top.

Roll out the remaining puff pastry dough thinly and mark with a lattice roller. Brush the edges of the dough shapes with egg yolk and stretch the lattice over the top of each one. Seal the edges and trim neatly. Leave to rest for 20 minutes.

Brush the lattice with egg yolk and bake at 375°F/190°C for about 15 minutes until golden brown. Dust with confectioners' sugar and glaze carefully under a hot broiler.

Add the Poire William to the vanilla sauce and warm gently. Place a pear on each plate and pour some sauce around.

SUMMER PUDDING

SHOWN IN ENGLISH
ON SAVOY MENUS

Line the base and sides of four dariole molds (page 166) with most of the bread by cutting it in ½-inch/1-cm wide fingers.

Simmer all the berries with the sugar over a moderate heat for about 10 minutes until the fruit is tender and the syrup is slightly reduced.

Pour the hot fruit and syrup into the bread-lined molds. Allow the bread to soak up the syrup, then add extra fruit as necessary to fill each mold

6 thin slices white bread, crusts removed
5 oz/150 g strawberries
5 oz/150 g blueberries
2 oz/50 g raspberries
2 oz/50 g red currants
¼ cup/50 g superfine sugar
1¼ cups/300 ml blackcurrant sauce (page 192)
heavy cream, whipped
4 wild strawberries
16 blueberries
12 raspberries
4 sprigs of red currants
4 sprigs of blackcurrants
confectioners' sugar

Serves 4

completely. Top each with a circle of bread slightly smaller than the mold. Cover and chill overnight. Unmold each summer pudding onto a plate. Spoon some blackcurrant sauce over each pudding and decorate with a rosette of cream and a wild strawberry.

Decorate each plate with four blueberries, three raspberries and a sprig of both red currants and blackcurrants dusted with confectioners' sugar.

TARTE
AUX ABRICOTS

APRICOT TART	12 fresh apricots, halved and stones removed	*Serves 8*
	2½ cups / 600 ml sugar syrup (page 204)	
	7 oz / 200 g sweet pastry dough (page 204)	
	2 oz / 50 g Genoese sponge (page 197)	
	2⅔ Tbsp / 40 ml kirsch	
	⅔ cup / 150 ml pastry cream (page 200)	
	19 whole almonds, roasted and skinned	
	¼ cup / 75 ml apricot jam, warmed and sieved	
	2 Tbsp / 25 g pistachio nuts, finely chopped	

Poach the apricot halves in the sugar syrup until just tender. Drain thoroughly and leave to cool.

Roll out the sweet pastry dough ⅛-inch / .3-cm thick and use to line an 8-inch / 20-cm flan ring or springform pan. Bake blind at 375°F / 190°C for about 20 minutes until lightly golden.

While still warm, transfer the tart shell to a plate. Leave to cool.

Arrange a thin layer of Genoese sponge on the base of the tart shell. Moisten with the kirsch. Top with a layer of pastry cream. Arrange the apricot halves, cut side up, in the tart shell, ensuring that the pastry cream is completely covered.

Cut small slices of the remaining apricots and arrange to finish the edge of the tart decoratively. Place a whole roasted almond in each apricot half. Lightly glaze with the warm jam. Decorate the edge of the tart with the chopped pistachio nuts.

TARTE BOURDALOUE

BOURDALOUE TART	7 oz/200 g sweet pastry dough (page 204)	*Serves 8*

Roll out the sweet pastry dough ⅛-inch/.3-cm thick and use to line an 8-inch/20-cm flan ring or springform pan. Trim the edges carefully.

Mix the ground almonds, flour, sugar and egg white to a smooth consistency. Melt the butter over a high heat until it turns nut brown in color, then quickly stir into the almond mixture. Stir in the Poire William.

Lightly poach the pears in the sugar syrup until just tender. Leave to cool, drain well and cut in half.

generous ⅔ cup/100 g blanched almonds, ground

3⅔ Tbsp/25 g all-purpose flour

½ cup/100 g superfine sugar

½ cup less 1 Tbsp/100 ml egg white

2 Tbsp/25 g unsalted butter

¼ cup/50 ml Poire William

4 small pears, peeled and cored

4 cups/1 liter sugar syrup (page 204)

2½ Tbsp/50 g apricot jam, warmed and sieved

confectioners' sugar

Spread the almond mixture over the bottom of the dough and arrange the pear halves on top, keeping the curved surfaces uppermost. Bake at 325°F/170°C for about 45 minutes until golden brown and just firm.

Remove the flan ring or pan and lightly glaze the surface with the apricot jam. Dust the edge of the tart with confectioners' sugar.

Serve immediately, accompanied by warm vanilla sauce (page 205).

TARTELETTE AUX PRUNEAUX, SABAYON A L'ORANGE

PLUM TARTLET WITH ORANGE SABAYON SAUCE		*Serves 4*
	7 oz/200 g puff pastry dough (page 200)	
	¼ cup/50 ml pastry cream (page 200)	
	10 oz/300 g plums, halved, pitted and thinly sliced	
	2½ Tbsp/20 g all-purpose flour	
	1⅓ Tbsp/15 g brown sugar	
	1 Tbsp/15 g chopped walnuts	
	ground cinnamon	
	1 Tbsp/15 g unsalted butter, melted	
	5 egg yolks	
	scant ⅓ cup/75 g superfine sugar	
	½ cup less 1 Tbsp/100 ml Sauternes	
	¼ cup/50 ml lemon juice	
	¼ cup/50 ml orange juice	

Roll out the puff pastry dough thinly and stamp out four 5-inch/12.5-cm circles. Place on a buttered baking sheet, prick thoroughly with a fork and leave to rest in the refrigerator for 30 minutes.

Spread a thin layer of pastry cream on top of each dough circle. Neatly fan the plum slices out onto the dough circles.

Mix the flour, brown sugar, wal-nuts, a generous pinch of cinnamon and the butter together. Sprinkle over the plums and bake at 350°F/180°C for about 20 minutes until golden brown.

Beat together the egg yolks, superfine sugar, Sauternes and lemon and orange juices over boiling water to form a light, fluffy sabayon. Spoon a little onto each warm plate.

Place the tartlets in the center of the orange sabayon.

TULIPE DE SORBET
AUX FRUITS D'ETE

**TULIP BASKET FILLED WITH
SUMMER FRUITS AND SORBET**

3 oz/75 g tuile mixture (page 205)
¼ cup/25 g slivered almonds
½ lb/225 g summer berries to include raspberries, loganberries, wild strawberries, blackberries and blueberries
1 cup less 2 Tbsp/200 ml raspberry sauce (page 201)
¼ cup/50 ml vanilla sauce (page 205)
2 Tbsp/25 ml mango sauce (page 198)
6 sprigs of red currants
6 sprigs of blackcurrants
confectioners' sugar
1 cup/250 ml strawberry sorbet (page 201)
4 sprigs of mint

Serves 4

Place an eight-pointed 5-inch/12.5-cm wide star-shaped plastic stencil on a buttered and floured baking sheet. Spread a little tuile mixture in the center and draw a spatula evenly over the surface. Remove the stencil and make three more stars in the same way.

Sprinkle a few slivered almonds in the center of each star. Bake at 375°F/190°C for 4–5 minutes until light brown. While still hot, place each tuile in a small glass bowl to form a tulip basket. Leave in the bowls until cold and crisp.

Divide the raspberry sauce between four plates. Pipe three large spots of vanilla sauce around the edge of each plate. Top each vanilla spot with a small spot of mango sauce. With a toothpick, draw through the spots of sauce to give a leaf-shaped effect. Place a sprig of red currant or blackcurrant dusted with confectioners' sugar between each.

Place a tulip basket in the center of each plate and fill with the prepared fruit. Pipe some sorbet into the center of each tulip basket and decorate with a sprig of mint.

Note: The sorbet in the photograph was made with elder flowers. As these are only available in early summer, strawberry sorbet is given in the recipe.

FEUILLETE
AUX FRUITS ROUGES

SUMMER FRUITS IN A PASTRY LEAF	9 oz / 250 g puff pastry dough (page 200)	*Serves 4*
	1 egg yolk, beaten	
	⅔ cup / 150 ml pastry cream (page 200)	
	½ cup less 1 Tbsp / 100 ml raspberry sauce (page 201)	
	5 oz / 150 g raspberries	
	5 oz / 150 g wild strawberries	
	confectioners' sugar	
	1 cup less 2 Tbsp / 200 ml vanilla sauce (page 205)	
	2⅔ Tbsp / 40 ml kirsch	
	2 Tbsp / 25 ml orange sauce (page 200)	
	4 sprigs of mint	

Roll out the puff pastry dough to ¼-inch / .5-cm thick and cut out four leaf shapes. Place on a buttered baking sheet and leave to rest in the refrigerator for 30 minutes.

Brush lightly with egg yolk. Using a small, sharp knife, score a line about ¼ inch / .5 cm in from the edge of each leaf. Mark the inner part with the back of a knife to give a criss-cross pattern. Bake at 400°F / 200°C for about 20 minutes until golden brown.

Carefully remove the lid with a knife and keep to one side. Scoop out any uncooked dough from the center.

Mix the pastry cream with half the raspberry sauce, warm gently, then fill each pastry case with some of this mixture. Arrange the raspberries and wild strawberries on top, ensuring that the pastry cream is completely covered. Dust the edge of each pastry lid with a little confectioners' sugar and place at an angle on top of the fruit.

Warm the vanilla sauce and add the kirsch. Pour a thin layer onto each plate. Position a filled pastry case in the center of each plate. Pipe three large dots of the remaining raspberry sauce on each plate. Pipe a small dot of orange sauce in the center and, using a toothpick, feather through each dot several times. Decorate each *feuilleté* with a sprig of mint.

PETITE TARTE DESMOISELLES TATIN

APPLE UPSIDE-DOWN TART

½ cup/100 g superfine sugar
1¾ cups/400 ml water
2 tsp/10 g glucose
7 medium dessert apples, peeled and cored
juice of ½ lemon
ground cinnamon
¼ cup/50 g unsalted butter
¼ lb/100 g puff pastry dough (page 200)
4 sprigs of apple mint

Serves 4

Cook the sugar, water and glucose in a heavy-bottomed saucepan to a pale amber color. Put a little of this caramel on to the base of four individual ramekins (about 3½-inches/9-cm wide and 1½-inch/4-cm high).

Slice the apples thinly and sprinkle with the lemon juice and a little cinnamon. Fill the ramekin dishes with the sliced apple and bake at 350°F/180°C for about 15 minutes until soft and reduced.

Sauté the remaining apple in the butter. Top up the ramekin dishes with this mixture and leave to cool.

Roll out the puff pastry dough ⅛-inch/.3-cm thick and cut into four circles slightly larger than the top of each ramekin. Prick the puff pastry dough with a fork and leave to rest for 20 minutes.

Cover the ramekins of apple with the dough circles and bake at 375°F/190°C for 20 minutes.

Leave to cool slightly before turning each one onto a plate. Surround with warm vanilla sauce and decorate with sprigs of apple mint.

REINETTE EN CHAUSSON,
BEURRE AU CALVADOS

**APPLE WRAPPED IN PASTRY
WITH CALVADOS BUTTER**

½ cup/75 g golden raisins
2 Tbsp/25 ml Calvados
4 Reinette apples
ground cinnamon
10 oz/300 g puff pastry dough (page 200)
1 egg yolk, beaten
½ cup/50 g confectioners' sugar
¼ cup/50 g superfine sugar
¼ cup/50 ml water
2 tsp/10 g glucose
¼ cup/50 g unsalted butter
⅔ cup/150 ml heavy cream

Serves 4

Soak the golden raisins in the Calvados for at least 1 hour. Drain, reserving the Calvados. Top and tail the apples so they stand level. Sprinkle the golden raisins with the cinnamon and use to fill the center of each apple.

Roll out the puff pastry dough ⅛-inch/.3-cm thick. Cut four ovals about 7 × 5-inches/18 × 12.5-cm and brush the edges with egg yolk. Enclose an apple in each oval of puff pastry dough. Seal the edges well and crimp with a small knife. Brush each one with egg yolk and make a small cut in the top. Bake at 375°F/190°C for about 20 minutes. Remove from the oven and dust generously with confectioners' sugar. Place under a hot broiler to give a nice shiny glaze.

Cook the superfine sugar, water and glucose in a heavy-bottomed saucepan to a pale amber color. Stir in the butter and the cream, reserving 2 Tbsp/25 ml, then add the reserved Calvados. Pass through a fine strainer.

Position each apple on a warm plate and surround with the sauce. Feather with the reserved cream.

PARFAIT DE THE
AU COULIS DE CAFE

TEA PARFAIT WITH COFFEE SAUCE

2 egg yolks
2½ Tbsp / 25 g superfine sugar
2 Tbsp / 25 ml Marsala
¼ cup / 50 ml sugar syrup (page 204)
1 tsp / 5 ml Earl Grey tea
2½ cups / 600 ml heavy cream
¼ cup / 50 ml raspberry sauce (page 201)
2 oz / 50 g semisweet couverture chocolate, tempered (page 204)
⅔ cup / 150 ml coffee sauce (page 195)
2 Tbsp / 25 ml chocolate sauce (page 194)
4 sprigs of mint

Serves 4

Beat the egg yolks, sugar and Marsala over boiling water to form a light, fluffy sabayon. Pass through a fine strainer and leave to cool.

Heat the sugar syrup and infuse the tea leaves. Leave to cool and pass the syrup through a fine strainer.

Reserve ½ cup less 1 Tbsp / 100 ml of the cream. Fold the tea syrup into the sabayon and remaining cream. Spoon this mixture into a half circle sleeve mold lined with plastic wrap. Level the surface, cover with plastic wrap and freeze for 3–4 hours.

Unmold the parfait. Whip the reserved cream. Fold the raspberry sauce into two-thirds of the cream and spread over the parfait. Pull a comb scraper across the raspberry cream to give a lined effect. Freeze for a further 30 minutes.

Fill a small wax paper piping bag with the tempered chocolate and pipe several designs of small tea and coffee pots onto baking parchment or wax paper. Leave to set.

Cut the parfait in neat portions with a sharp, warm knife. Pour a little coffee sauce onto each plate. Position a slice of parfait in the center of each plate. Pipe five large dots of chocolate sauce around each plate and add a dot of coffee sauce on top of each one. Draw through the dots with a toothpick. Decorate the top with a small rosette of the reserved whipped cream and a sprig of mint. Position the coffee and tea pot designs in the cream.

VEGETABLE ACCOMPANIMENTS AND GARNISHES

CHOU FRISE
A LA CREME

SAVOY CABBAGE WITH CREAM	This dish is shown in the photograph on page 150	Serves 4–6

Remove the outside leaves from the cabbage and discard. Cut the cabbage in quarters, discard the stem and shred very finely. Blanch in boiling salted water for about 4 minutes, refresh and squeeze out excess moisture.

1 × 1¾ lb/750 g Savoy cabbage
2½ oz/65 g bacon, cut in *julienne*
1⅓ Tbsp/20 g unsalted butter
1¼ cups/300 ml heavy cream
salt and freshly milled pepper

Blanch the bacon for 30 seconds and refresh. Melt the butter and fry the bacon until crisp. Drain thoroughly. Reduce the cream by half and add the cabbage and bacon. Warm gently. Season to taste.

POMMES SAVOYARD

SAVOY POTATOES	This dish is shown in the photograph on page 121	Serves 4

Slice the potatoes about ⅛-inch/.3-cm thick, then dry thoroughly on a dish towel.

Heat the oil and toss the potato slices very quickly to blanch them. Season generously and arrange neatly in four

2 cups/300 g potatoes, cut in small cylinders
2 Tbsp/25 ml oil
1⅓ Tbsp/20 g unsalted butter
salt and freshly milled pepper

buttered 4-inch/10-cm round non-stick pans.

Place directly over a high heat for 2–3 minutes to brown the bottoms, then bake at 400°F/200°C for about 20 minutes or until tender. Unmold.

TIMBALE DE BROCCOLI

BROCCOLI TIMBALE	This dish is shown in the photograph on page 111	Serves 10

Dry the broccoli on a dish towel, then chop roughly. Reduce the cream by two-thirds, then leave to cool. Add the cream to the broccoli. Purée, then pass through a fine strainer.

Beat the egg and egg yolk and add to

1 medium stalk/200 g broccoli, cooked
1 cup less 2 Tbsp/200 ml heavy cream
1 egg and 1 egg yolk
salt and freshly milled pepper

the broccoli mixture. Season to taste.

Pour the mixture into buttered timbale molds, (about 1½-fl oz/40-ml capacity) and poach in a water bath at 200°F/100°C for about 35 minutes until just firm. Unmold.

TURNING VEGETABLES

Cut the vegetables in even-sized oblongs, then trim to elongated barrel shapes.

WILD MUSHROOMS

Scrape the stems clean with a small knife, then trim the bottoms of the stems. Wash thoroughly just before using. Keep small mushrooms whole; cut larger ones in half.

PREPARING VEGETABLE 'SPAGHETTI'

The vegetables are prepared using a special blade of a mandolin. If cutting by hand, the vegetables should be cut in strips similar to pasta spaghetti.

ONION PIQUE

Peel a small onion and stud it with a fresh bay leaf and 2 whole cloves.

CREPES AUX MAIS ET POIVRONS

CORN AND PEPPER PANCAKES	This dish is shown in the photograph on page 136	Serves 4

Blanch the corn-on-the-cob in boiling salted water for 6 minutes and refresh. Carefully remove the corn kernels from the cob and dry them thoroughly.

Sweat the diced red and green pepper in 1 Tbsp/15 g of the butter in a covered pan for about 5 minutes until tender, then drain thoroughly.

Mix the cream with the flour and egg yolks, then stir in the corn and

1 corn-on-the-cob
heaped ¼ cup/40 g finely diced red pepper
heaped ¼ cup/40 g finely diced green pepper
2⅔ Tbsp/40 g unsalted butter
½ cup less 1 Tbsp/100 ml heavy cream
3⅔ Tbsp/25 g all-purpose flour
3 egg yolks
¼ cup/50 ml oil
salt and freshly milled pepper

peppers. Season with salt and pepper.

Heat half the oil and half the remaining butter in a large skillet. Place six metal rings about 2-inches/5-cm in diameter in the pan. Fill the metal rings about ½-inch/1-cm deep with the mixture. Fry until golden on one side, remove the rings, turn the pancakes and fry until golden on the other side. Repeat until all the mixture is used.

NAVETS A LA DAUPHINOISE

TURNIPS WITH CREAM	This dish is shown in the photograph on page 138	Serves 4

Cut the turnips in paper-thin slices, sprinkle generously with salt and leave for about 1 hour in a cool place.

Squeeze the slices of turnip in a dish towel until thoroughly dry. Season

14 oz/400 g small turnips, peeled
1 cup less 2 Tbsp/200 ml heavy cream
salt and freshly milled pepper

with pepper and arrange in a buttered ovenproof dish. Bring the cream to a boil and pour over the turnips. Bake at 350°F/180°C for about 45 minutes until tender.

TIMBALE DE BETTERAVES

BEET TIMBALE	This dish is shown in the photograph on page 74	Serves 10

Dry the beet on a dish towel, then chop roughly. Mix the cream and beet together. Purée, then pass through a fine strainer. Beat the eggs, add to the beet mixture and season to taste.

3 cooked beets/150 g (2-inch/5-cm diameters)
½ cup less 1 Tbsp/100 ml heavy cream
2 eggs
salt and freshly milled pepper

Pour the mixture into buttered timbale molds (about 1½-fl oz/40-ml capacity) and poach in a water bath at 200°F/100°C for 35 minutes until just firm. Unmold.

TOMATO FILLETS

Cut plum tomatoes in quarters, cut out the seeds and carefully cut as close as possible to the skin to remove the flesh.

TOMATO ROSE

Using a serrated knife, cut a continuous spiral strip from a firm tomato, starting at the base. Keeping the skin-side outside, roll into a tight flower shape.

TURNING MUSHROOMS

1 Using a small, pointed paring knife, score the mushrooms from the center to the edge at regular intervals, removing a narrow strip of flesh each time. Discard the stems. 2 Turned mushrooms.

CHOU ROUGE BRAISE

BRAISED RED CABBAGE	This dish is shown in the photograph on page 150	Serves 10

3 lb/1.5 kg red cabbage, thinly sliced
1 cup less 2 Tbsp/200 ml red wine
¼ cup/50 ml red-wine vinegar
scant ½ cup/50 g sliced onion
heaped ¼ cup/65 g goose fat or unsalted butter
2 Tbsp/25 g brown sugar
1¾ cups/400 ml chicken stock (page 194)
1 clove
60 peppercorns
2 eating apples, peeled, cored and sliced
½ cup/100 g fresh apple purée
½ cup less 1 Tbsp/100 ml dry white wine
salt and freshly milled pepper

Season the cabbage with salt and pepper and marinate in the red wine and red-wine vinegar for 4 hours.

Sweat the onion in the goose fat until transparent, add the sugar and sweat until well glazed. Add the cabbage with its marinade and the chicken stock and transfer to an oven-proof dish. Wrap the clove and peppercorns in cheesecloth and add to the cabbage mixture.

Cover and braise at 325°F/170°C for 40 minutes. Stir occasionally. Add the apple slices, apple purée and white wine to the cabbage. Braise for a further 30–40 minutes or until the cabbage is tender and all the liquid has evaporated. Remove from the oven, discard the cheesecloth bag and season to taste.

SPETZLI

EGG NOODLES WITH SPINACH	This dish is shown in the photograph on page 142	Serves 4

3¼ cups/400 g all-purpose flour
6 eggs
2 Tbsp/25 g spinach purée (page 193)
2 Tbsp/25 ml oil
grated nutmeg
2⅔ Tbsp/40 g unsalted butter
salt and freshly milled pepper

Mix half the flour with three of the eggs, the spinach purée, half the oil, nutmeg, salt and pepper to a very elastic dough. Beat with a wooden spoon until air bubbles develop. Mix the remaining flour, eggs and oil with the seasonings in the same way.

Bring a large saucepan of salted water with a dash of oil to a boil. Spread a small amount of either dough thinly on a thin wooden board, about 10 × 8-inches/25 × 20-cm. Dip the whole board into the boiling water and then, using a spatula, quickly scrape off small strips of the dough directly into the boiling water. Cook for about 1 minute, then refresh. Repeat until both doughs are used up.

Melt the butter and toss the spetzli until warm. Season to taste.

SULFRINO BALLS

Using a *sulfrino* cutter, scoop small balls from firm vegetables.

VEGETABLE DIAMONDS

CABBAGE BALLS

1 Remove the outside leaves of a Savoy cabbage and discard. Cut in quarters and remove stems. Blanch the leaves. 2 Take one or two leaves at a time and form into a ball by squeezing tightly in cheesecloth.

POLENTA

FRIED CORNMEAL DIAMONDS	This dish is shown in the photograph on page 133	*Serves 10*

Bring the water to a boil, add a pinch of salt and sprinkle in the cornmeal slowly, stirring constantly. Cook over a very gentle heat for about 20 minutes, stirring frequently.

Turn the mixture onto a generously

2¼ cups/500 ml water
1 cup/120 g fine cornmeal
2⅔ Tbsp/40 g unsalted butter
salt

oiled baking sheet and level the surface. Cover and cool in the refrigerator for at least 2 hours.

Cut in neat diamond shapes. Melt the butter and fry the polenta diamonds until golden brown.

GNOCCHI ALLA ROMANA

FRIED SEMOLINA HALF-MOONS	This dish is shown in the the photograph on page 118	*Serves 10*

Bring the milk to a boil, then add ¼ cup/50 g of the butter and a pinch of salt. Pour in the semolina, stirring constantly, and cook over a low heat for 15 minutes. Leave to cool slightly, then add the egg yolks and grated Parmesan. Pour the mixture onto a buttered baking sheet and refrigerate

2¼ cups/500 ml milk
5 Tbsp/75 g unsalted butter
¾ cup/100 g semolina
2 egg yolks, beaten
5 Tbsp/25 g grated Parmesan
¼ cup/50 ml oil
salt

for 2–3 hours.

Stamp out half-moon shapes and fry in the remaining butter and oil until golden brown.

Alternatively, sprinkle with extra grated Parmesan and lightly brown under a hot broiler.

TIMBALE D'ASPERGES

ASPARAGUS TIMBALE	This dish is shown in the photograph on page 60	*Serves 10*

Dry the asparagus with a dish towel, then chop roughly.

Reduce the cream by two-thirds and leave to cool. Add the cream to the asparagus. Purée, then pass through a fine strainer.

Beat the egg and the egg yolk and

heaped 1⅓ cups/200 g cooked asparagus trimmings
1 cup less 2 Tbsp/200 ml heavy cream
1 egg and 1 egg yolk
grated nutmeg
salt and freshly milled pepper

add to the asparagus mixture. Season to taste with nutmeg, salt and pepper.

Pour the mixture into buttered timbale molds (about 1½-fl oz/40-ml capacity) and poach in a water bath at 200°F/100°C for about 35 minutes until just firm. Unmold.

VEGETABLE
PAYSANNE

VEGETABLE
JULIENNE

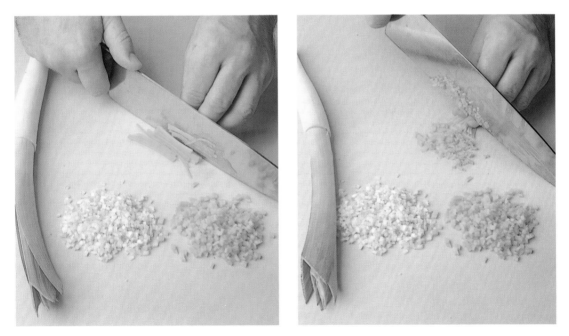

VEGETABLE
BRUNOISE

RÖSTI DE PANAIS ET CAROTTES

PARSNIP AND CARROT RÖSTI	This dish is shown in the the photograph on page 148	Serves 4

Sweat the carrot in 1⅓ Tbsp/20 g of the butter for about 2 minutes until tender. Sweat the parsnip in 1⅓ Tbsp/20 g of the butter for about 6 minutes until tender.

Combine the carrot and parsnip

scant 1 cup/100 g grated carrot
6 Tbsp/90 g unsalted butter
1 cup/100 g grated parsnip
1 egg yolk
salt and freshly milled pepper

with the egg yolk and season generously. Divide the mixture in four and shape each portion into a small, flat cake. Melt the remaining butter and fry the cakes until golden brown on both sides.

LEGUMES VARIES ROYAL

VEGETABLE MEDLEY	This dish is shown in the the photograph on page 121	Serves 4

Cut all the vegetables except the lima beans in dice and season to taste.

Mix the cream with the egg yolk and season generously. Then stir all the vegetables into the cream mixture and use to fill four small buttered molds or

1½-inch/4-cm piece of medium carrot, cooked *al dente*
scant ½ cup/40 g cauliflower flowerets, cooked *al dente*
½ cup/40 g broccoli flowerets, cooked *al dente*
scant ½ cup/40 g French green beans, cooked *al dente*
2¼-inch/6-cm piece of medium zucchini, cooked *al dente*
2 Tbsp/25 g shelled lima beans, cooked *al dente*
½ cup less 1 Tbsp/100 ml heavy cream
1 egg yolk
salt and freshly milled pepper

egg cups.

Cover and poach in a water bath at 300°F/150°C for about 20 minutes or until just firm.

Unmold and serve with a selection of fresh vegetables.

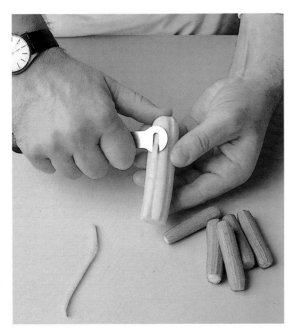 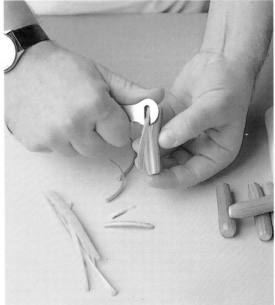

TO CANALE

Using a *canalé* knife, score grooves at close regular intervals in the skin of vegetables, such as zucchini and cucumbers and fruit, such as lemons and oranges, which gives a decorative effect, particularly when sliced.

VEGETABLE BATONS

BASIC RECIPES AND PREPARATION TECHNIQUES

It is advisable to make up the basic recipes in the given quantities; any surplus can usually be refrigerated or frozen.

BECHAMEL SAUCE

2⅔ Tbsp/40 g unsalted butter

5⅓ Tbsp/50 g all-purpose flour

5 cups/1.25 liters milk

1 onion piqué (page 181)

salt and freshly milled pepper

Melt the butter in a saucepan, add the flour and work together to make a roux. Cook without coloring for 5–6 minutes over a low heat, then leave to cool. Bring the milk just to a boil with the onion piqué. Add the milk to the roux slowly, stirring all the time. Cook slowly over a low heat for about 30 minutes. Pass through a fine strainer and season to taste.

BEEF STOCK

2¼ lb/1 kg beef bones

12 white peppercorns, crushed

1 onion, unpeeled and cut in half

2 cups/100 g sliced leek

1 cup/100 g sliced celery

½ bay leaf

1 sprig of thyme

2 large parsley stems

1 clove of garlic

salt

Place the beef bones in a saucepan and just cover with cold water. Bring to a boil slowly, skimming frequently. Add the peppercorns and salt. Simmer very gently for about 2 hours.

Brown the onion halves in a heavy-bottomed pan. Add to the stock with the remaining ingredients. Simmer for a further hour, then pass through cheesecloth and skim off the fat.

BEURRE BLANC

1 Tbsp/10 g chopped shallot

6 white peppercorns, crushed

2 Tbsp/25 ml white-wine vinegar

1 cup less 2 Tbsp/200 ml dry white wine

2 Tbsp/25 ml heavy cream

10 Tbsp/150 g unsalted butter, chilled and diced

cayenne

salt

Place the shallot, white peppercorns, vinegar and white wine in a saucepan and reduce by half. Add the cream and reduce until the mixture thickens. Remove from the heat and work in the butter. Season with cayenne and salt and pass through a fine strainer. Keep warm over hot water.

Beurre au cerfeuil: Use herb vinegar instead of white-wine vinegar. Add a few chervil stems to the reduction. Add a sprinkling of chopped chervil to the finished sauce.

Beurre au citron: Halve the amount of vinegar and make up to 2 Tbsp/25 ml with lemon juice.

Beurre au citronelle: Halve the amount of vinegar and make up to 2 Tbsp/25 ml with fresh lime juice.

BLACKCURRANT SAUCE

2 cups/250 g blackcurrants

⅔ cup/150 ml sugar syrup (page 204)

Purée the blackcurrants and sugar syrup in a blender or food processor. Pass through a fine strainer.

PREPARING A CHICKEN BREAST

1 Remove the mignon fillet from the halved boneless breast and discard the sinews. **2** Carefully cut horizontally almost through the breast. **3** Open out flat. **4** Place both pieces of chicken between sheets of plastic wrap and beat out flat.

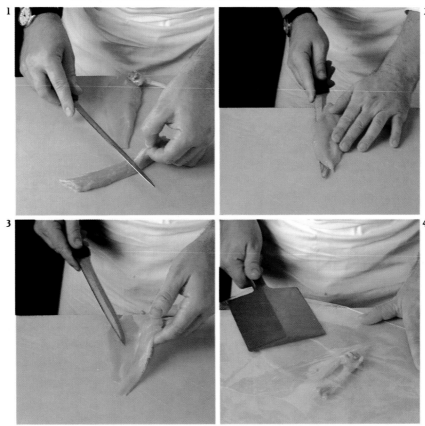

CANNOISE

⅔ cup/100 g chopped onion

¼ cup/50 g unsalted butter

½ cup less 1 Tbsp/100 ml vegetable oil

1 clove of garlic, crushed

2 Tbsp/20 g tomato paste

1 cup/150 g diced plum tomato fillets

⅔ cup/100 g finely cubed red pepper

⅔ cup/100 g finely cubed green pepper

½ cup/100 g diced egg plant

generous ½ cup/50 g diced green zucchini

generous ½ cup/50 g diced yellow zucchini

salt and freshly milled pepper

Sweat the onion in the butter and half the oil slowly until transparent. Add the garlic and sweat for a further 1 minute. Add the tomato paste and the tomatoes, season with salt and pepper and simmer for about 5 minutes.

Season the remaining vegetables with salt and pepper, heat the remaining oil and toss them very quickly, then add to the tomatoes. Cover and cook at 350°F/180°C for about 20 minutes. Remove from the oven and season to taste.

CARAMELIZED ORANGE JULIENNE

finely pared peel of 2 medium oranges, cut in *julienne*

1 cup less 2 Tbsp/200 ml water

scant ⅔ cup/120 g superfine sugar

Poach the orange *julienne* gently in the water until tender. Add the sugar and dissolve over a moderate heat. Bring to a boil and boil gently for 5 minutes. Leave to cool in the syrup.

Store in the syrup until required. Drain well before using.

CARROT PUREE

1⅛ lb/500 g carrots

2⅔ Tbsp/40 g unsalted butter

salt and freshly milled pepper

Steam the carrots until tender. Purée in a food processor or blender. Pass through a fine strainer, place in a saucepan and cook over a moderate heat, stirring frequently until any excess liquid has evaporated. Stir in the butter and season with salt and pepper.

Any root vegetable may be prepared in the same way.

Spinach purée: Blanch the spinach, then proceed as above.

CHICKEN ASPIC

1 pig's trotter

1⅛ lb/500 g chicken legs

1 cup/100 g mirepoix (page 207)

2 egg whites

5½ cups/1.5 liters chicken stock (page 194)

bouquet garni

salt and freshly milled pepper

Place the pig's trotter in cold salted water, bring to a boil, then refresh under cold, running water.

Bone out the chicken legs, chop the bones and coarsely grind the meat. Combine with the mirepoix, egg whites, cold

PREPARING MEDALLIONS FROM A SADDLE OF LAMB

1 Pull off the skin. 2 Using a sharp knife, cut down the length of the backbone. 3 Ease the meat from the bones on either side. 4 Trim the fat and cut in medallions about 1½-inch/4-cm thick.

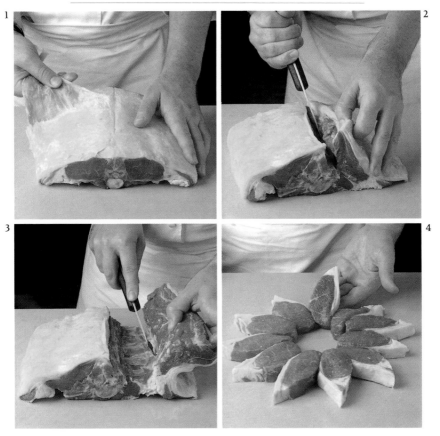

chicken stock and pig's trotter. Add the bouquet garni and salt and pepper. Bring to a boil slowly, stirring occasionally with a metal spoon. As soon as a froth forms on top of the stock, stop stirring and simmer over a very gentle heat for 1 hour. Season to taste. Pass through fine cheesecloth, leave to cool and refrigerate until set.

The pig's trotter should release enough strength to set the aspic.

Duck aspic with port:
Prepare as above, but with duck stock (see next recipe) and duck legs. Add ½ cup less 1 Tbsp/100 ml of ruby port to each 4 cups/1 liter of prepared aspic.

CHICKEN STOCK

1 boiling fowl, dressed

1⅛ lb/500 g chicken bones (if available)

12 white peppercorns, crushed

1 sprig of thyme

a few parsley stems

½ bay leaf

1 cup/100 g chopped celery

2 cups/100 g chopped leek

heaped ¼ cup/50 g chopped carrot

1 small onion, unpeeled and halved

salt and freshly milled pepper

Choose a saucepan not much larger than the chicken. Just cover the chicken and bones with about 5½ cups/1.5 liters cold water. Bring to a boil slowly and skim off all the fat. Add the peppercorns, herbs, celery, leek, carrot and salt.

Brown the onion halves in a heavy-bottomed pan and add to the stock. Simmer until the chicken is tender, then remove from the saucepan. Season to taste, then pass the stock through a fine strainer or cheesecloth.

For strong chicken stock, reduce by fast boiling to half the amount.

Duck stock: Prepare as above, but with duck legs and duck bones.

CHOCOLATE SAUCE

1¼ cups/100 g cocoa powder

1¼ cups/300 ml water

1 cup less 2 Tbsp/225 g superfine sugar

2 oz/50 g semisweet couverture chocolate, tempered (page 204)

Mix the cocoa powder to a paste with a little of the water. Dissolve the sugar in the remaining water over a low heat. Stir in the cocoa paste and bring to a boil, stirring constantly. Remove from the heat and add the chocolate to the sauce, stirring constantly until blended. Pass through a fine strainer.

CHOUX PASTRY DOUGH

½ cup/120 ml milk

¼ cup/50 g unsalted butter

7 Tbsp/65 g all-purpose flour, sifted

2 eggs

salt

Boil the milk with the butter until the butter is melted.

PREPARING CHICKEN LEGS

1 Cut the skin around the drumstick just above the knuckle. Twist the knuckle to remove and pull away the sinews.   2 Loosen the thigh bone by easing around the flesh with a sharp knife.   3 Twist the joint and remove the bone. 4 Make an incision in the thigh skin and push the drumstick through to make a neat shape.

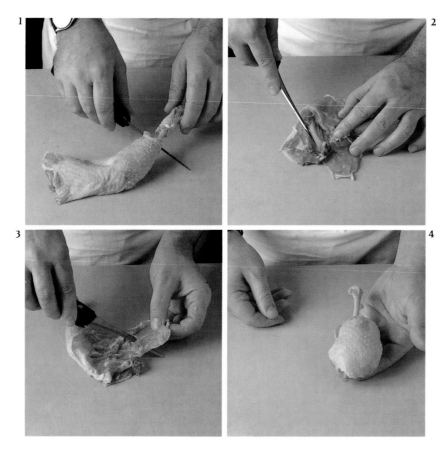

Reduce the heat, add the flour and salt and stir well until the mixture forms a smooth paste. Cook, stirring, for 2–3 minutes. Transfer to a bowl and beat in the eggs, one at a time.
Yield 9 oz/250 g

COFFEE SAUCE

2⅔ Tbsp/10 g ground coffee

2¼ cups/500 ml vanilla sauce (page 205)

Infuse the coffee in the warm vanilla sauce for 20 minutes. Pass through a fine strainer or cheesecloth and leave to cool.

COURT BOUILLON

2 cups/100 g thinly sliced leek (white part only)

1 cup/100 g thinly sliced celery

⅔ cup/100 g thinly sliced carrot

1 cup/65 g thinly sliced button mushrooms

1 cup/100 g thinly sliced fennel

scant ¾ cup/65 g minced shallot

2 Tbsp/25 g unsalted butter

¼ cup/50 ml white-wine vinegar

1 cup less 2 Tbsp/200 ml dry white wine

8 cups/2 liters water

bouquet garni

½ clove of garlic

salt

Sweat the vegetables in the butter. Add the vinegar, white wine and water. Simmer for 10 minutes, then add the bouquet garni, garlic and salt. Simmer for a further 10 minutes, remove from the heat and pass through fine cheesecloth.

CROUTONS

4 slices white bread, cut in ¼-inch/.5-cm thick slices

½ cup less 1 Tbsp/100 ml oil

¼ cup/50 g unsalted butter

Remove the crusts from the bread and cut into batons about ¼-inch/.5-cm wide and ¾-inch/2-cm long. Heat the oil and butter together and toss the bread batons until golden brown. Drain on paper towels.

CUMBERLAND SAUCE

2 oranges

1 lemon

2 Tbsp/25 g unsalted butter

sugar

½ cup less 1 Tbsp/100 ml water

1 Tbsp/10 g chopped shallot

12 peppercorns, crushed

1¾ cups/400 ml ruby port

¼ cup/50 ml red-wine vinegar

1 cup less 2 Tbsp/200 ml chicken stock (page 194)

⅔ cup/200 g red currant jelly

ground ginger

Pare the peels from the oranges and lemon, blanch and refresh. Melt about one-fifth of the butter in a saucepan, add a generous pinch of sugar and caramelize lightly. Add the orange and lemon peels and water. Reduce. Squeeze the juice

PREPARING SCALLOPS

1 Place the scallop rounded-side down on the work surface. Using a round-bladed knife, ease the shell all the way around. Pull hard to separate the two half shells. 2 Remove the scallop from its shell by loosening with a knife. 3 Cut around the solid white muscle and discard any membrane. Reserve the coral roe and wash thoroughly. 4 Wash and trim the scallop, then cut in half.

from the oranges and lemon and add to the saucepan with the shallot, peppercorns, port, red-wine vinegar, chicken stock, red currant jelly and a pinch of ginger. Simmer for about 10 minutes until the sauce begins to thicken slightly. Pass through a fine strainer and stir in the remaining butter.

FISH MOUSSE

1⅛ lb/500 g white fish fillets such as sole, skinned

2 egg whites

1¾ cups/400 ml heavy cream

cayenne

salt and freshly milled pepper

Season the fish fillets with salt and pepper, and refrigerate for at least 1 hour. Dry the fish on a dish towel and mince or work in a food processor until smooth. Place a fine strainer over a bowl set in ice, then pass the fish through the strainer. Add the egg whites gradually and work in thoroughly. Add the cream slowly and continue mixing over the ice until all the cream is incorporated. Season with cayenne, salt and pepper.

FISH STOCK

2¼ lb/1 kg sole or turbot bones

4 Tbsp/40 g chopped shallot

1⅓ Tbsp/20 g unsalted butter

1 cup less 2 Tbsp/200 ml dry white wine

4 cups/1 liter water

1 cup/50 g sliced leeks

½ cup/50 g sliced celery

12 white peppercorns

½ bay leaf

2 large/10 g parsley stems

¼ cup/20 g mushroom trimmings

salt and pepper

Chop the fish bones and wash well in cold water. Sweat the shallots in the oil, add the fish bones, cover and cook for about 3 minutes. Add the white wine, water and the remaining ingredients. Bring to a boil and simmer for about 15 minutes, skimming frequently. Pass through fine cheesecloth and skim off any remaining fat.

FLEURONS

1½ oz/40 g puff pastry dough (page 200)

1 egg yolk, beaten

poppy seeds

sesame seeds

Roll the puff pastry dough ⅛-inch/.3-cm thick, ensuring that it is rolled in different directions to prevent distortion when cooking.

Using a 2½-inch/6-cm fluted cutter, stamp out four crescent-shaped pieces. Place on a buttered baking sheet. Brush the tops with egg yolk and sprinkle with a few poppy and sesame seeds. Leave to rest in the refrigerator for 20 minutes. Bake at 400°F/200°C for 15 minutes until golden brown.

Other shapes such as fish or stars can be made in the same way. (See wild mushroom fleurons, page 206.)

FRANGIPANE

8 Tbsp/120 g unsalted butter

generous ½ cup/120 g superfine sugar

2 eggs, beaten

scant 1 cup/120 g blanched almonds, ground and sifted

3⅔ Tbsp/25 g all-purpose flour, sifted

Cream the butter and sugar until pale using a mixer on high speed. Add the eggs slowly until well incorporated. Fold in the almonds and flour.

GAME STOCK

1⅛ lb/500 g game trimmings and bones such as venison, pheasant or quail

1⅓ Tbsp/20 g unsalted butter

scant 1¼ cups/120 g mirepoix (page 207)

1 cup less 2 Tbsp/200 ml red wine

5½ cups/1.5 liters chicken stock (page 194)

1 bay leaf

1 sprig of thyme

12 peppercorns, crushed

salt

Roast the game trimmings and bones with the butter at 425°F/220°C for about 20 minutes until browned. Add the mirepoix and roast for a further 10 minutes. Discard the fat. Add the red wine, chicken stock, herbs and peppercorns, and simmer for about 45 minutes, skimming frequently so that the stock remains clear. Season with salt. Pass through a fine strainer or cheesecloth.

GAZPACHO COULIS

1 lb 5 oz/600 g plum tomatoes, chopped

6-inch/15-cm piece of cucumber, pared and seeds removed

⅓ cup/40 g of both chopped red and green pepper

⅔ cup/100 g chopped onions

½ clove of garlic, chopped

¼ cup/10 g fresh white bread crumbs

2 Tbsp/25 ml olive oil

¼ cup/50 ml white-wine vinegar

SHAPING QUENELLES

1 Using two tablespoons or teaspoons (depending on the size required) dipped in water, take a spoonful of mousse and transfer it from one spoon to the other until a perfect quenelle is formed. 2 Place on wax paper.

3⅓ Tbsp/50 ml tomato catsup

1¾ cups/400 ml chicken stock (page 194)

freshly chopped oregano

¼ cup/50 ml mayonnaise (page 199)

salt and freshly milled pepper

Place all the vegetables in a bowl with the bread crumbs, oil, vinegar, catsup, chicken stock, a sprinkling of oregano, and salt and pepper. Cover and marinate for 24 hours.

Purée in a blender or food processor and stir in the mayonnaise. Pass through a fine strainer, season to taste.

GENOESE SPONGE

⅔ cup/150 ml beaten eggs (4–5 eggs)

½ cup plus 5 tsp/120 g superfine sugar

1 cup plus 1½ Tbsp/120 g flour, sifted

2 tsp/10 g unsalted butter, melted

Butter and line an 8-inch/20-cm round cake pan. Beat the eggs and sugar in a bowl over simmering water until the mixture has increased in volume and the beater leaves a trail. Fold in the flour and melted butter. Transfer the mixture to the prepared pan and bake at 350°F/180°C for about 35 minutes until risen and firm to the touch. Cool on a wire rack.

HOLLANDAISE SAUCE

½ cup less 1 Tbsp/100 ml dry white wine

¼ cup/50 ml white-wine vinegar

½ cup less 1 Tbsp/100 ml water

12 white peppercorns, crushed

1 Tbsp/10 g chopped shallots

stems of chervil, parsley and tarragon

5 egg yolks

2⅔ cups/600 g unsalted butter

juice of ½ lemon

salt and freshly milled pepper

Place the white wine, vinegar, water, peppercorns, shallot and a few herb stems in a saucepan over a moderate heat. Reduce by two-thirds and leave to cool. Pass through a fine strainer and add to the egg yolks. Beat in a water bath or over very hot water with a balloon whisk until the mixture coats the back of a spoon. Melt the butter slowly and skim the white sediment from the top. Leave to cool to blood temperature (98.4°F/36.8°C).

Beat the butter slowly into the egg mixture. Season with lemon juice, salt and pepper.

JUS DE VEAU

5 pieces of veal bone

scant 1⅓ cups/200 g roughly chopped carrots

heaped 1 cup/200 g roughly chopped onions

scant 4 cups/200 g roughly chopped leek

1¾ cups/200 g roughly chopped celery

1 calf's foot

1 clove of garlic, chopped

10 Tbsp/100 g tomato paste

1¼ cups/300 ml white wine

1 Tbsp/10 g peppercorns, crushed

a few sprigs of thyme

2 bay leaves

⅓ cup/100 g tomato trimmings

salt and freshly milled pepper

Place the veal bones in a large saucepan of cold water and bring to a boil. Drain and wash well under cold, running water. Return the bones to the pan, add half the vegetables and cover with cold water. Simmer for about

COCKS' COMBS

Blanch by placing in cold salted water and bringing to a boil. Drain and refresh. Place in a dish towel with some coarse salt and rub vigorously to remove the fine outer skin. Trim off the feathery base. Cook in stock for about 30 minutes or until tender.

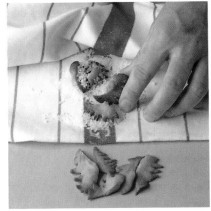

4 hours, then strain. Discard the bones.

Chop the calf's foot and roast at 425°F/220°C until lightly browned. Add the remaining vegetables, garlic and tomato paste. Roast for 15–20 minutes, stirring occasionally. Add the white wine, prepared stock, peppercorns, herbs and tomato trimmings. Simmer gently, skimming frequently. Reduce by half and pass through a fine strainer or cheesecloth. Season to taste.

Glace de viande: Reduce the jus de veau by boiling to a very thick, dark, syrupy glaze.

LIME SAUCE

finely pared peel of 1 lime, cut in *julienne*

¼ cup/50 g superfine sugar

1¾ cups/400 ml water

2 Tbsp/15 g arrowroot

2¼ cups/500 ml fresh lime juice

Poach the lime *julienne* in a little water until tender. Drain and reserve.

Dissolve the sugar in the water and bring to a boil. Mix the arrowroot and lime juice together. Stir into the boiling liquid and cook until thickened. Leave to cool, then pass through a fine strainer or cheesecloth. Stir in the reserved *julienne*.

LOBSTER MOUSSE

⅓ cup/50 g uncooked lobster meat

½ egg white

½ cup less 1 Tbsp/100 ml heavy cream

¼ egg yolk

salt and freshly milled pepper

Dry the lobster meat thoroughly with a dish towel. Season with salt and leave to rest in the refrigerator for at least 20 minutes. Dry the lobster meat again, then mince or work in a food processor.

Set a small bowl in a bowl of ice. Pass the lobster through a fine strainer into the chilled bowl. Slowly add the egg white, then slowly stir in the cream, keeping the bowl over ice all the time. Add the egg yolk and season. The consistency should be almost runny at this stage. Leave to rest in the refrigerator for about 25 minutes or until the mixture becomes slightly firm.

LOBSTER SAUCE

2 Tbsp/25 ml oil

1⅛ lb/500 g lobster shells, finely crushed (page 201)

⅓ cup/65 g chopped onions

1⅓ cups/65 g chopped leek

1 clove of garlic, chopped

5 Tbsp/65 g plum tomato fillets, chopped

4 Tbsp/40 g tomato paste

1 cup less 2 Tbsp/200 ml dry white wine

4 cups/1 liter chicken stock (page 194)

12 peppercorns, crushed

a few sprigs of tarragon

2¾ cups plus 1 Tbsp/650 g unsalted butter

cayenne

salt and freshly milled pepper

Heat the oil and fry the shells quickly. Add the onion, leek, garlic, tomato and tomato paste, and fry for a further 5 minutes. Add the white wine, chicken stock, peppercorns and tarragon, and simmer for 30 minutes, skimming frequently. Pass through a fine strainer or cheesecloth. Reduce by four-fifths. Cut the butter in small pieces and add one by one to the sauce over a low heat. Season with cayenne, salt and pepper.

PRESERVING FRESH TRUFFLES

1 Scrub the truffles with a vegetable brush.   2 Place whole or thinly sliced in a preserving jar.   3 Cover with port and seal. The liquid in the jar is the truffle juice referred to in several of the recipes.

MADEIRA SAUCE

4 Tbsp/40 g chopped shallots

4⅓ Tbsp/65 g unsalted butter

24 black peppercorns, crushed

1 sprig of thyme

¼ cup/50 ml Madeira

¼ cup/50 ml truffle juice (page 198)

4 cups/1 liter jus de veau (page 197)

Sweat the shallots in ¼ cup/50 g of the butter. Add the peppercorns, thyme, Madeira and half the truffle juice. Reduce by two-thirds and add the jus de veau. Simmer for about 10 minutes, skimming frequently. Add the remaining truffle juice and season to taste. Pass through a fine strainer and stir in the remaining butter.

MANGO SAUCE

3 medium-sized, ripe mangoes

juice of ½ lemon

½ cup less 1 Tbsp/100 ml sugar syrup (page 204)

Peel the mangoes and remove the flesh from around each stone. Blend to a smooth consistency. There should be about 1¾ cups/400 ml of purée. Add the lemon juice and sugar syrup. Mix thoroughly, then pass through a fine strainer or cheesecloth.

MAYONNAISE

4 egg yolks

¼ cup/50 ml white-wine vinegar

4 tsp/20 g Dijon mustard

Worcestershire sauce

4 cups/1 liter vegetable oil

salt and freshly milled pepper

Combine the egg yolks, vinegar and mustard with a dash of Worcestershire sauce and salt and pepper in a food processor and mix well. Add the oil while the machine is working until it has all been incorporated and the mayonnaise is thick. Season to taste.

MUSHROOM DUXELLE

4¼ cups/300 g quartered button mushrooms

2 Tbsp/25 g unsalted butter

¼ cup/50 ml dry white wine

½ cup less 1 Tbsp/100 ml heavy cream

1½ Tbsp/15 g chopped shallot

salt and freshly milled pepper

Sweat the mushrooms in three-quarters of the butter, add the white wine and season to taste. Remove from the pan when cooked and chop very finely. Reduce the mushroom stock to a glaze, add the cream and reduce by half. Sweat the shallot in the remaining butter until transparent, add the mushrooms and cream and season to taste.

NOODLE DOUGH

4¼ cups/500 g all-purpose flour

2 Tbsp/25 ml oil

4 eggs

4 egg yolks

salt and freshly milled pepper

Mix all the ingredients together thoroughly until they form a smooth dough. Cover and leave to rest for at least 20 minutes in the refrigerator before using.

To prepare noodles, roll out the dough as thinly as possible on a surface sprinkled with semolina. Cut into an oblong. Fold each short end in toward the center, then fold in once more to meet in the center. Turn the dough over and cut in very thin strips. Lift the noodles with a knife to separate them. Cook in boiling water with a dash of olive oil until *al dente*. *Yield* 1¾ lb/750 g

BEET NOODLE DOUGH

4¼ cups/500 g all-purpose flour

2 Tbsp/25 ml oil

3 eggs

3 egg yolks

⅓ cup/50 g beet purée (page 193)

Proceed as above.

PREPARING OYSTERS

1 Push an oyster knife into the hinged section of the oyster.   2 Twist the knife to open the oyster.   3 Ease the knife between the oyster and the flat side of the shell to release it. Loosen the oyster from the shell. If used for cooking, remove the beard and the small, round hard muscle.

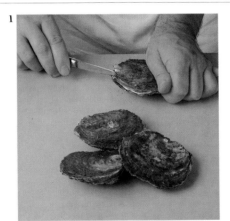

SPINACH NOODLE DOUGH

4¼ cups/500 g all-purpose flour

2 Tbsp/25 ml oil

3 eggs

3 egg yolks

heaped ⅓ cup/50 g spinach purée (page 193)

Proceed as above.

ORANGE DRESSING

juice of 1 orange

2 Tbsp/25 ml sherry vinegar

1 tsp/5 ml Dijon mustard

sugar

1 cup less 2 Tbsp/200 ml olive oil

salt and freshly milled pepper

Reduce the orange juice by half and leave to cool. Mix the vinegar and mustard with a pinch of sugar. Beat in the oil slowly, then beat in the orange juice. Season to taste.

ORANGE SAUCE

2 Tbsp/15 g arrowroot

2¼ cups/500 ml orange juice

2⅔ Tbsp/40 g superfine sugar

¼ cup/50 ml Grand Marnier

Mix the arrowroot with a little of the cold orange juice. Dissolve the sugar in the remaining orange juice over a moderate heat. Add the arrowroot to the boiling orange juice and stir gently until thickened. Leave to cool,

then pass through a fine strainer and add the Grand Marnier.

PALMIERS

7 oz/200 g puff pastry dough (page 200)

¼ cup/50 ml sugar syrup (page 204)

¼ cup/50 g superfine sugar

Roll out the puff pastry dough to an oblong about ¼-inch/.5-cm thick. Brush with the sugar syrup and sprinkle with half the superfine sugar. Fold both short sides to meet in the center, then fold in half. Leave to rest for about 20 minutes in the refrigerator. Cut in ¼-inch/.5-cm thick slices.

Sprinkle a buttered baking sheet with half the remaining sugar and place the slices on top. Sprinkle with the remaining sugar and bake at 425°F/220°C for about 5 minutes. Then turn each slice over carefully and bake for a further 5 minutes. Cool on a wire rack.

PASTRY CREAM

2½ cups/600 ml milk

1 vanilla bean, split

4 egg yolks

scant ⅓ cup/75 g superfine sugar

½ cup plus 1 Tbsp/75 g all-purpose plain flour, sifted

Bring the milk to a boil over a low heat with the split vanilla bean. Beat the egg yolks and sugar together well until pale and creamy. Add the flour and mix to a smooth paste. Pour on half the boiling milk and mix well. Return to the saucepan with the remaining milk, stirring constantly, and boil for 1 minute. Pass through a fine strainer.

PASTRY DOUGH FOR PATE EN CROUTE

1½ cups plus 2⅔ Tbsp/200 g all-purpose flour

½ cup plus 2 Tbsp/120 g unsalted butter, chilled

1 egg, beaten

¼ cup/50 ml milk

¼ cup/50 ml water

salt

Sift the flour with a pinch of salt. Cut in the butter until the mixture resembles fine crumbs. Stir in the beaten egg, milk and water, and mix to a smooth dough. Refrigerate until ready to use.
Yield 1 lb/450 g

PILAF RICE

1 Tbsp/10 g minced onion

¼ cup/50 ml oil

1 heaped cup/200 g Patna rice

2¼ cups/500 ml vegetable stock (page 206)

1 bay leaf

salt and freshly milled pepper

Sweat the onion in the oil until transparent. Add the rice and stir until it is completely coated with oil. Add the boiling vegetable stock and the bay leaf. Season with salt and pepper. Cover and cook at 350°F/180°C for 20 minutes, or until tender. *Saffron rice:* Add a pinch of saffron strands with the stock.

PUFF PASTRY DOUGH

3 cups/675 g unsalted butter

5¾ cups/675 g all-purpose flour

1–1½ tsp/5–7 g salt

1 cup plus 2 Tbsp/275 ml water, chilled

juice of ½ lemon

Work together 2¼ cups/500 g of the butter with 1¼ cups/175 g of the flour on a cool surface. When well mixed, form into a block 5-inches/12.5-cm square and 1½-inches/4-cm deep and refrigerate.

Cut the remaining butter into the remaining flour with the salt until the mixture resembles fine bread crumbs. Add the chilled water and lemon juice to form a dough, and mix until smooth and elastic.

Shape the dough into a

USING A TRELLIS CUTTER

1 Roll out the dough thinly and cut into an oblong. Roll the trellis cutter along the length of the doughs. 2 Carefully ease open to give a lattice effect.

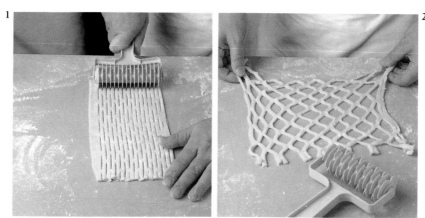

small ball, then make two incisions to one-third of the depth to form a cross.

Open out the points and roll out each one to about ¼-inch/.5-cm thick, 5-inches/12.5-cm wide and 5-inches/12.5-cm long. Place the butter and flour block in the center of the dough and fold the flaps over anti-clockwise, ensuring that the edges are well sealed. Roll the dough into a 12 × 24-inch/30 × 60-cm oblong. Fold the short sides to meet in the middle, then fold in half to form four equal layers; this is called a double-turn. Cover with a damp cloth and leave to rest in the refrigerator for at least 30 minutes. Repeat the process four times, then leave the dough, covered, in the refrigerator to rest, preferably overnight.

Yield 2½ lb/1.25 kg

RASPBERRY SAUCE

10 oz/300 g raspberries

2 tsp/10 ml lemon juice

⅓ cup/40 g confectioners' sugar

Purée the raspberries in a blender, then add the lemon juice and confectioners' sugar. Pass through a fine strainer.

SALAD DRESSING

3⅓ Tbsp/50 g Dijon mustard

⅔ cup/150 ml white-wine vinegar

3½ cups less 2 Tbsp/800 ml olive oil

superfine sugar

salt and freshly milled pepper

Mix the mustard and vinegar together. Add the oil, stirring constantly. Season with sugar, salt and pepper.

SAVORY PIE CRUST DOUGH

¼ cup/50 g unsalted butter, cut in small dice

¼ cup/50 g lard, cut in small dice

1½ cups plus 2⅔ Tbsp/200 g all-purpose flour

7 tsp/35 ml water

salt

Cut the butter and lard into the flour with a pinch of salt until the mixture resembles fine bread crumbs. Add the water and quickly mix to a smooth dough. It is important to avoid over-mixing as this will produce a tough pastry. Cover and leave to rest in the refrigerator.

Yield ¾ lb/350 g

SAVOY DRESSING

2⅔ Tbsp/40 ml red-wine vinegar

2 tsp/10 g Dijon mustard

½ clove of garlic, crushed

2⅔ Tbsp/40 ml sugar syrup (page 204)

Worcestershire sauce

Tabasco sauce

¼ cup/50 ml olive oil

2 Tbsp/25 ml soy sauce

1½ Tbsp/15 ml tomato catsup

1-inch/2.5-cm piece of leek, cut in *brunoise* and blanched

¾-inch/1.5-cm piece of carrot, cut in *brunoise* and blanched

salt and freshly milled pepper

Beat the vinegar, mustard, garlic and sugar syrup together. Add Worcestershire sauce, Tabasco, salt and pepper to taste. Gradually beat in the olive oil, soy sauce and tomato ketchup. Season to taste and stir in the vegetable *brunoise*.

STRAWBERRY SAUCE

14 oz/400 g strawberries

½ cup/50 g confectioners' sugar

Purée the strawberries and sugar in a blender. Pass through a fine strainer.

STRAWBERRY SORBET

9 oz/250 g strawberries

⅔ cup/150 ml water

½ cup/100 g superfine sugar

2 tsp/10 ml lemon juice

Purée all the ingredients in a blender or food processor. Pass through a fine strainer or cheesecloth. Freeze in a *sorbetière*. Alternatively, freeze

in a rigid container, then work in a food processor.

STUFFING FOR QUAIL

2 oz/50 g chicken livers

½ cup less 1 Tbsp/100 ml milk

1 Tbsp/10 g chopped shallot

¼ cup/50 g unsalted butter

1 eating apple, peeled, cored and sliced

1 Tbsp/10 g dried morels, soaked in cold water for at least 1 hour

1 oz/25 g lean pork, cut in cubes

¾ oz/20 g pork belly, cut in cubes

2 oz/50 g veal, cut in cubes

½ egg, beaten

2 Tbsp/25 ml Madeira

salt and freshly milled pepper

Marinate the chicken livers in the milk overnight, then wash and dry.

Sweat the shallots in half the butter until transparent. Add the apple slices. Drain and dry the morels, then sweat in the remaining butter, season to taste and leave to cool. Finely grind the lean pork, pork belly and veal twice or finely chop in a food processor. Mince the apple and shallot mixture and the chicken livers. Add to the ground meats, mix well and mix in the egg. Reduce the Madeira, add to the mixture. Pass through a fine strainer. Season generously.

CRUSHING SHELLS

1 Place the shells in a large bowl.   2 Crush with the end of a rolling pin until quite fine. Small quantities may be crushed in a mortar and pestle.

REMOVING THE SHELL FROM A LOBSTER

1 Twist off the two large claws.   2 Twist the head to separate it from the tail.   3 Lay the tail on its side and press firmly to crack the undershell.   4 Carefully peel away the shell.   5 Twist the large claws at the first joint to separate them from the knuckle.   6 Tap both ends on the work surface to loosen the flesh.   7 Break off the small pincer claw and ease out the flesh.   8 Using a sharp knife, carefully cut away the side of the shell, then crack the claw around the center and carefully pull apart to release the flesh.   9 Cut the lobster tail in angled slices.   10 The prepared lobster.

PREPARING ORANGE SEGMENTS

1 Using a serrated knife, cut off the top and base of the orange, then work down the side, removing the skin and pith in sections.   2 Carefully ease the segments from the membrane.

SUGAR SYRUP

2½ cups/500 g superfine sugar

4 cups/1 liter water

¼ cup/50 ml lemon juice

Dissolve the sugar in the water over a moderate heat. Add the lemon juice and bring to a boil. Leave to cool, strain and use as required.

SWEET PASTRY DOUGH

1 cup/225 g unsalted butter

½ cup/100 g superfine sugar

1 egg, beaten

3 cups less 1 Tbsp/350 g all-purpose flour

salt

Cream the butter and sugar together until very pale. Slowly beat in the egg. Slowly add the flour with a pinch of salt and mix to a smooth dough. Cover and leave to rest in the refrigerator for at least 1 hour.

TEMPERING CHOCOLATE

Cut the required amount of couverture chocolate in small pieces. Melt in a water bath over a very low heat. Do not allow the water to become too hot as any steam would spoil the chocolate. (Water is couverture's worst enemy.) Heat the chocolate to 122°F/50°C.

Cool the chocolate in a water bath containing cold water. Using a plastic spatula, scrape the cooling chocolate from the edges and bottom of the bowl and stir constantly to ensure the chocolate remains smooth. Reduce the temperature of the chocolate to 82°F/28°C. At this temperature the chocolate should be thickening.

Raise the temperature to 86°F/30°C in a water bath containing warm water. At this stage of preparation the temperature should not exceed 86°F/30°C. If it does, the chocolate should be cooled again to 82°F/28°C and brought back slowly to 86°F/30°C. At that temperature the chocolate should be smooth, slightly thickened but still pourable.

Before using the chocolate, test it by dipping the end of a spatula into the chocolate and refrigerating until set. Touch the chocolate lightly with your thumb. If the chocolate melts immediately, it has not been correctly tempered and the process must be repeated.

REMOVING THE TAIL SHELL FROM LANGOUSTINE AND CRAYFISH

1 Using scissors, make an incision in the under-surface, starting at the tail. **2** Cut along the length of the tail on both sides and carefully peel back the shell. **3** Using a toothpick, loosen the tail meat.

TOMATO COULIS

⅓ cup/40 g minced onion

1 clove of garlic, chopped

4⅓ Tbsp/65 g unsalted butter

14 oz/400 g plum tomatoes, quartered

4 Tbsp/40 g tomato paste

6 basil leaves with stems

½ cup less 1 Tbsp/100 ml vegetable stock (page 206)

salt and freshly milled pepper

Sweat the onion and garlic in 1⅓ Tbsp/20 g of the butter until transparent. Add the tomatoes and tomato paste with the basil stems and vegetable stock and simmer gently for about 20 minutes until the tomatoes are thoroughly cooked. Pass through a fine strainer. Return to the heat and reduce to the desired consistency. Season to taste, add the chopped basil leaves and stir in the remaining butter.

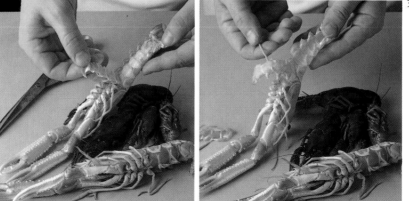

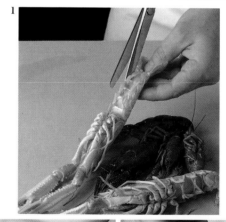

TUILE MIXTURE

1 cup less 1 Tbsp/100 g all-purpose flour

1 cup/100 g confectioners' sugar

½ cup/100 g unsalted butter, melted

2 egg whites

Sift the flour and confectioners' sugar into a mixing bowl. Quickly stir in the melted butter and egg whites to make a smooth dough. Refrigerate for 30 minutes. Then spread the mixture into a stencil to form the desired shape, such as a tulip (see Tulipe de Sorbet aux Fruits d'Eté, page 172).

VANILLA ICE CREAM

⅓ cup/25 g milk powder

2¼ cups/500 ml milk

1¼ cups/300 ml heavy cream

1 vanilla bean, split

5 egg yolks

½ cup/100 g superfine sugar

Mix the milk powder to a thick paste with a little of the milk. Stir in the remaining milk. Add the milk to the cream and bring to a boil with the split vanilla bean. Allow to infuse for 15 minutes. Beat the egg yolks and sugar together, pour the infused milk on top and mix well.

Transfer the mixture to a clean saucepan and cook over a very gentle heat, stirring all the time with a wooden spoon until the sauce becomes thick and coats the back of the spoon. It is important not to boil the mixture at this stage – otherwise it will separate. Cool and pass through a fine strainer.

Freeze in an ice cream machine to a light consistency. Store in the freezer for 2 hours until firm and ready to scoop.

Alternatively, freeze in a rigid container until ice crystals begin to form. Beat well or work in a food processor until smooth. Freeze for at least 4 hours or until required.

VANILLA SAUCE

2¼ cups/500 ml milk

1 vanilla bean

6 egg yolks

5 Tbsp/75 g superfine sugar

Heat the milk and infuse the vanilla bean in it for about 10 minutes. Beat the egg yolks and sugar together. Bring the milk to a boil, pour onto the egg yolk mixture and mix thoroughly. Place the mixture in a clean pan and stir gently with a wooden spoon over a low heat until the sauce thickens and coats the back of the spoon. Leave to cool, then pass through a fine strainer.

VANILLA SPONGE SHEET

2½ cups/600 ml beaten eggs

¼ cup/50 ml egg yolks

2 cups/400 g superfine sugar

2 cups plus 2⅔ Tbsp/250 g flour, sifted

Butter and line two large baking sheets. Beat the beaten eggs and yolks with the sugar in a mixer set at high speed for 7 minutes, then at slow speed for 3 minutes. Fold in the flour. Spread a thin layer of the mixture on to the prepared sheets and bake immediately at 450°F/230°C for about 5 minutes. Leave to cool on the sheet, then gently peel off the lining paper.

BONING OUT A DUCK

1 Remove the wishbone.   **2** Using a filleting knife and starting at the head end, work as closely as possible to the carcass, easing the flesh from the bone to remove it completely. Take care not to pierce the skin.   **3** Bone out the legs and wings in a similar way.

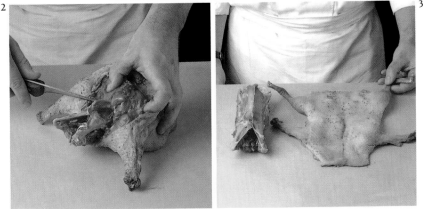

VEAL MOUSSE

¼ lb/100 g very lean veal

1 egg white

1 cup less 2 Tbsp/200 ml heavy cream

salt and freshly milled pepper

Finely grind the veal or mince in a food processor. Position a fine strainer over a bowl set in ice. Pass the veal through the strainer. Add the egg white and stir in thoroughly, with the bowl still set over the ice, until the mixture feels very stiff. Add the cream slowly, stirring constantly. Season generously with salt and pepper.

Chicken mousse: Use lean chicken meat to replace the veal.

VEGETABLE STOCK

½ cup/50 g chopped shallots

¼ cup/50 g unsalted butter

scant 2 cups/300 g sliced carrots

3½ cups/200 g sliced leeks

2 cups/200 g sliced fennel

1¾ cups/200 g sliced celery

2 cups/200 g sliced celery root

1 cup less 2 Tbsp/200 ml dry white wine

24 white peppercorns, crushed

5½ cups/1.5 liters chicken stock (page 194)

salt and freshly milled pepper

Sweat the shallots in the butter, then add all the remaining vegetables. Sweat for about 6 minutes in a covered pan. Season with salt and pepper and add the white wine, peppercorns and chicken stock. Simmer for about 30 minutes, then pass through a fine strainer or cheesecloth.

WHITE WINE SAUCE

1 Tbsp/10 g chopped shallots

12 white peppercorns, crushed

½ cup less 1 Tbsp/100 ml dry white wine

1 cup less 2 Tbsp/200 ml fish stock (page 196)

½ cup less 1 Tbsp/100 ml vegetable stock (page 206)

½ cup less 1 Tbsp/100 ml heavy cream

cayenne

salt

Place the shallot, peppercorns and white wine in a saucepan and reduce by two-thirds. Add the fish and vegetable stocks and reduce again by two-thirds. Add the heavy cream and reduce by half. Season to taste with the cayenne and salt.

WILD MUSHROOM FLEURONS

1 Tbsp/10 g minced shallot

1⅓ Tbsp/20 g unsalted butter

heaped ½ cup/40 g assorted wild mushrooms, cleaned

2 Tbsp/25 ml ruby port

2 Tbsp/25 ml truffle juice (page 198)

1½ oz/40 g puff pastry dough (page 200)

1 egg yolk

salt and freshly milled pepper

JOINTING A CHICKEN

1 Remove the legs. 2 Cut through the skin where the wing and breast join and scrape the meat from the wing bone. 3 Separate at the first joint. 4 Remove the wishbone. 5 Remove the skin from the breast, if necessary, and carefully remove the breast from the carcass.

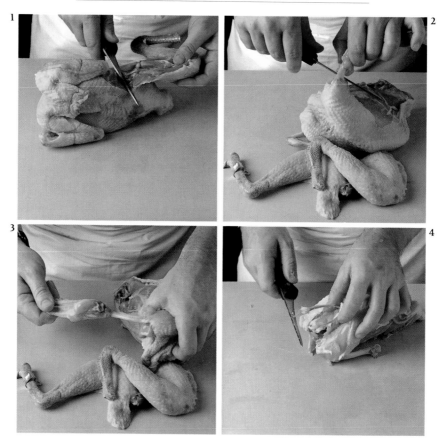

Sweat the shallot in the butter until transparent.

Cut the wild mushrooms in ¼-inch/.5-cm cubes, add to the shallots and sweat for a further 5 minutes. Season with salt and pepper and remove from the saucepan. Add the port and truffle juice to the saucepan and reduce.

DRYING LOBSTER EGGS

Hold the live lobster firmly in one hand and, using a spoon, scrape the eggs from the under-surface around the tail fins. Blanch the eggs in boiling salted water, drain and refresh, then dry thoroughly. Place on a dish and leave in the oven at lowest setting until dried.

Stir in the mushrooms. Season to taste and leave to cool.

Roll out the puff pastry dough about ⅛-inch/.3-cm thick and stamp out twenty

1½-inch/4-cm circles. Brush the edges with egg yolk. Divide the mushroom mixture between half the dough circles and cover with the remaining circles. Seal the edges well. Brush with egg yolk and leave to rest for about 20 minutes. Bake at 400°F/200°C for 15 minutes until golden brown.

GLOSSARY

BREAD FLUTE

A thin French bread stick similar to a baguette.

CULINARY TERMS

Al dente: Usually applied to vegetables and pasta which are slightly undercooked and so remain crisp.

Blanch: Usually a preliminary stage of cooking. Plunge food in cold or boiling water, bring quickly to the boil and cook for a short time. Drain and refresh to prevent further cooking. Vegetables are usually blanched in boiling water to retain their color, meat and bones in cold water. Food can also be blanched without coloring by plunging in moderately hot oil.

Déglace: To dilute the concentrated juices in a saucepan or roasting pan in which meat, poultry, game or fish has been fried, braised or roasted. Wine, fortified wine or stock are usually used for this purpose.

Reduce: To reduce the volume of a liquid by evaporation by boiling in an uncovered saucepan. Used to thicken a sauce and concentrate the flavor.

Refresh: To plunge in iced water until cold. Used to retain the color of vegetables or to halt the cooking process.

Sweat: To cook food, usually vegetables, very gently in a mixture of butter and oil without coloring until tender.

EGG FILLETS

Shell a hard-boiled egg and using a vegetable parer, peel off thin strips. Cut as required.

GRIOTTINE CHERRIES

Wild morello cherries commercially preserved in a light brandy syrup.

HERBS (deep-fried)

Wash and thoroughly dry fresh herbs or leaves such as parsley, sage, basil, rosemary or celery. Dip in very hot oil for 2 seconds and remove. Drain on a dish towel.

LEAF GELATIN

Soak leaves of gelatin in cold water for about 15 minutes to soften. Drain and dissolve in stock or sugar syrup over a low heat.

MIREPOIX

A mixture of finely diced vegetables to include equal quantities of leek, celery, carrot and onion, flavored with a few peppercorns, a bay leaf and a sprig of thyme.

White mirepoix: A mixture of the white part of a leek, celery and onion, flavored as above.

PISTACHIOS AND WALNUTS (to remove skins)

Just cover the nuts with milk and bring to a boil. Remove the skin while warm.

QUAILS' EGGS

For soft-boiled eggs, cook in boiling salted water for 2 minutes. Drain, refresh and shell.

REINETTE APPLE

A small French apple. Slightly

tart, it is used for both eating and cooking.

SHELLFISH (to cook)

Lobster   Plunge a 1 lb/450 g live lobster into boiling salted water and cook for 5 or 10 minutes, drain and refresh. Cook for 5 minutes if it is to be reheated in the recipe, for 10 minutes if it is to be served cold.

Crayfish: Cook in the same way for 2 minutes.

Langoustine: Cook in the same way for 3 minutes.

SNAILS

Good quality fresh snails are only available in the spring so use canned ones as an alternative.

SWEETBREADS

Place in cold salted water for about 2 hours to remove any blood, changing the water frequently. Place in a saucepan of cold water, bring to a boil, drain and refresh. Simmer in salted water with 1 onion piqué (page 181) for 40 minutes. Cool in the water. Remove the skin and membrane, and dry thoroughly.

COCKTAILS

Left to right TIP OF THE TONGUE; SAVOY AFFAIR

COCKTAILS

CHAMPAGNE COCKTAILS

CHAMPAGNE COCKTAIL

Put 1 lump, or 1 teaspoon, of sugar in a champagne glass and saturate it with Angostura bitters. Fill the glass with cold Champagne and serve with a slice of orange. Add a dash of brandy if desired.

FRAISE ROYALE

Crush 2 strawberries and top up with Champagne.

LADY OF MEY

Created in honor of the Queen Mother's 80th birthday.

1 fl oz passion fruit juice	
½ fl oz Cherry Heering	
½ fl oz brandy	

Shake and top up with Champagne.

MOONWALK

Created in honor of the intrepid astronauts.

1 fl oz Grand Marnier	
1 fl oz fresh grapefruit juice	
2 dashes of orange flower water	

Shake and pour into a champagne glass. Top up with Champagne.

PECHE ROYALE

Crush half a peach and top up with Champagne.

ROYAL SILVER

Created to celebrate the Silver Jubilee of Queen Elizabeth II.

½ fl oz Cointreau	
½ fl oz Poire William	
1 fl oz fresh grapefruit juice	

Top up with Champagne.

SAVOY AFFAIR

¼ fl oz fresh lime juice	
¼ fl oz passion fruit juice	
¼ fl oz Fraise de Bordeaux	
¼ fl oz peach liqueur	

Frost the rim of a glass with sugar. Shake the ingredients and top up with Champagne. Decorate with a sugar-frosted strawberry.

SAVOY 90

Created in 1979 to celebrate the Savoy's 90th anniversary.

¾ fl oz Amaretto	
¼ fl oz fresh lime juice	

Top up with Champagne.

SAVOY ROYALE

Crush 2 strawberries and half a peach and top up with Champagne.

SAVOY SPRINGTIME

¼ fl oz gin	
¼ fl oz Cointreau	
¼ fl oz fresh orange juice	

Shake, add a dash of fresh orange juice and top up with Champagne.

SUPER SAVOY

One of three cocktails created for British Airways when Concorde was launched.

½ Cointreau	
¼ fresh orange juice	
¼ Campari	

Top up with Champagne.

TIP OF THE TONGUE

⅓ fl oz Medori	
⅓ fl oz passion fruit juice	
⅓ fl oz gin	
dash of egg white	
dash of syrup	

Shake and strain into a glass. Top up with Champagne.

COCKTAILS

ALLIES COCKTAIL

Dating back to World War II when the American Bar was a favorite haunt of war correspondents.

½ dry gin	
½ dry vermouth	
2 dashes of Kummel	

Shake well and strain into a cocktail glass.

AMERICAN COCKTAIL

⅓ Campari	
⅔ sweet vermouth	
cube of ice	

Use a wine glass. Top up with soda water, stir and add a twist of lemon peel.

Left to right   MARGARET ROSE; DRY MARTINI; SEA BREEZE; FALLEN ANGEL; FROZEN DAIQUIRI

ANGEL FACE

⅓ dry gin

⅓ apricot brandy

⅓ apple brandy

Shake well and strain into a cocktail glass.

BETWEEN-THE-SHEETS COCKTAIL

1 dash of fresh lemon juice

⅓ brandy

⅓ Cointreau

⅓ Bacardi rum

Shake well and strain into a cocktail glass.

BLOODY MARY COCKTAIL

1½ fl oz vodka

2 fl oz tomato juice

½ fl oz fresh lemon juice

2 dashes of Worcestershire sauce

Shake and strain into a medium-sized wine glass.

BLUE HAWAIIAN

1 fl oz light rum

½ fl oz blue Curaçao

2 fl oz fresh pineapple juice

1 fl oz coconut cream

crushed ice

Blend and pour into a tall glass. Decorate with a slice of orange, a slice of lime and a maraschino cherry.

BULLSHOT COCKTAIL

1 fl oz vodka

4 fl oz beef bouillon or condensed consommé

1 dash of fresh lemon juice

2 dashes of Worcestershire sauce

celery salt

Shake and strain into a large glass.

CARUSO COCKTAIL

⅓ dry gin

⅓ dry vermouth

⅓ green Crème de Menthe

Shake well and strain into a cocktail glass.

DAIQUIRI COCKTAIL

1 teaspoon confectioners' sugar

¼ fresh lime juice

¾ Bacardi rum

Shake well and strain into a cocktail glass.

DEBUTANTE COCKTAIL

The name of this cocktail evokes memories of a vanished era when the London Season was strictly observed by both the aristocracy and those with social aspirations.

⅓ gin

⅓ fresh lemon juice

⅙ Crème de Noyaux

⅙ fresh lime juice

1 egg white

Shake and strain into a cocktail glass.

DRY MARTINI COCKTAIL

⅕ dry vermouth

⅘ dry gin

Stir well with ice and serve with a twist of lemon peel.

FALLEN ANGEL COCKTAIL

1 dash of Angostura bitters

2 dashes of green Crème de Menthe

juice of 1 lemon or ½ lime

2 fl oz dry gin

Shake well and strain into a cocktail glass. Decorate with a green maraschino cherry.

FROZEN DAIQURI COCKTAIL

juice of ½ lime

1 teaspoon confectioners' sugar

2 fl oz Bacardi rum

1 dash of Maraschino

Put into a blender with crushed ice and pour unstrained into a champagne glass. Add a maraschino cherry and serve with straws.

GREEN-EYED MONSTER COCKTAIL

⅓ dry gin

⅓ sweet vermouth

⅓ green Chartreuse

Stir with ice and strain into a cocktail glass.

HARVEY WALLBANGER COCKTAIL

1½ fl oz vodka

4 fl oz fresh orange juice

2 teaspoons Galliano

Layer in an ice-filled highball glass. Serve with straws.

INK STREET COCKTAIL

Ink Street represents Fleet Street, for many years the heart (sic) of British newspapers.

⅓ rye whiskey

⅓ fresh orange juice

⅓ fresh lemon juice

Shake well and strain into a cocktail glass.

IOLANTHE COCKTAIL

Appropriately named after one of Gilbert and Sullivan's most popular operas, first performed at the Savoy Theatre.

⅓ brandy

⅓ Lillet

⅙ Grand Marnier

⅙ fresh orange juice

3 dashes of orange bitters

Shake and strain into a cocktail glass.

Left to right MAI TAI; WHITE LADY; TEQUILA SUNRISE; BLUE HAWAIIAN

LEAP YEAR COCKTAIL

Created by Harry Craddock for the Leap Year celebrations at the Savoy on February 29 1928, this cocktail is reputed to have been responsible for more proposals than any other that has ever been mixed!

| 1 dash of fresh lemon juice |
| ⅔ gin |
| ⅙ Grand Marnier |
| ⅙ sweet vermouth |

Shake well and serve in a cocktail glass. Squeeze lemon peel on top.

MAGGIE BLUE

Created in honor of Margaret Thatcher's triumphant success in the 1979 General Election.

| ½ fl oz vodka |
| ¼ fl oz Framboise |
| ¾ fl oz fresh lime juice |
| 1 dash of gomme syrup |
| 1 dash of blue Curaçao |

Shake and serve in a cocktail glass.

MAI TAI COCKTAIL

| 1 fl oz white rum |
| 1 fl oz golden rum |
| ½ fl oz Curaçao |
| juice of 1 lime |
| 1 fl oz fresh pineapple juice |
| 3 dashes of gomme syrup |
| 1 dash of Grenadine |

Shake and pour into a large old-fashioned glass filled with ice. Decorate with a piece of pineapple, a maraschino cherry and a sprig of mint.

MANHATTAN COCKTAIL

| 1 dash of Angostura bitters |
| ⅔ rye whiskey |
| ⅓ sweet vermouth |

Stir well and strain into a cocktail glass. Serve with a maraschino cherry.

MARGARET ROSE COCKTAIL

Named after Princess Margaret who was always called Margaret Rose as a little girl.

| ⅓ dry gin |
| ⅓ Calvados |
| ⅙ Cointreau |
| ⅙ fresh lemon juice |
| 1 dash of Grenadine |

Shake well and strain into a cocktail glass.

MERRY WIDOW COCKTAIL

| 2 dashes of Pernod |
| 2 dashes of Angostura bitters |
| 2 dashes of Bénédictine |
| ½ dry vermouth |
| ½ dry gin |

Stir well and strain into a cocktail glass. Twist lemon peel on top. The original version of this cocktail contained absinthe but Pernod is now used.

MIKADO COCKTAIL

Another cocktail emphasizing the D'Oyly Carte connection.

| 2 dashes of Angostura bitters |
| 2 dashes of Crème de Noyau |
| 2 dashes of Orgeat syrup |
| 2 dashes of Curaçao |
| 1 fl oz brandy |

Shake well and strain into a cocktail glass.

MILLION DOLLAR COCKTAIL

One of the cocktails included in the first edition of *The Savoy Cocktail Book* when a million dollars represented a fortune.

| 1 tablespoon fresh pineapple juice |
| 1 teaspoon Grenadine |
| 1 egg white |
| ⅓ sweet vermouth |
| ⅔ gin |

Shake well and strain into a medium-sized glass.

OLD-FASHIONED COCKTAIL

| 1 lump, or 1 teaspoon, of sugar |
| 2 dashes of Angostura bitters |
| 2 fl oz rye whiskey |

Crush the sugar and bitters together in a medium-sized glass. Add the whiskey, a cube of ice and decorate with a twist of lemon peel, a slice of orange and a maraschino cherry. This cocktail can be made with other spirits if liked.

PINA COLADA

| 1 fl oz white rum |
| 1 fl oz dark rum |
| 2 fl oz fresh pineapple juice |
| 1 fl oz coconut cream |
| 1 dash of fresh lime juice |
| crushed ice |

Blend and pour into a tall glass. Decorate with a slice of lime, a piece of pineapple and a maraschino cherry. Serve with straws.

ROB ROY COCKTAIL

| 1 dash of Angostura bitters |
| ⅓ sweet vermouth |
| ⅔ Scotch whisky |

Stir well and strain into a cocktail glass.

ROLLS-ROYCE COCKTAIL

| ⅓ brandy |
| ⅓ Cointreau |
| ⅓ fresh orange juice |

Shake well and strain into a cocktail glass.

SCREWDRIVER COCKTAIL

| ⅓ vodka |
| ⅔ fresh orange juice |

Shake well and strain into a long glass. Add ice and a slice of orange.

Left to right GOLDEN CADILLAC; GRASSHOPPER; UNION JACK; WHITE RUSSIAN

SEA-BREEZE

½ vodka

⅙ dry vermouth

⅙ blue Curaçao

⅙ Galliano

Stir and strain into an ice-filled old-fashioned glass. Decorate with a slice of orange.

SIDECAR

¼ fresh lemon juice

¼ Cointreau

½ brandy

Shake well and strain into a cocktail glass.

TANGO COCKTAIL

Named after the dance beloved by the Bright Young Things, as they were popularly known, who found the music of the Savoy Orpheans irresistible.

2 dashes of Curaçao

juice of ¼ orange

¼ dry vermouth

¼ sweet vermouth

½ dry gin

Shake well and strain into a cocktail glass.

TEQUILA SUNRISE

1 fl oz Tequila

4 fl oz fresh orange juice

2 dashes of Grenadine

Layer the Tequila and orange juice in an ice-filled old-fashioned glass and stir. Add the Grenadine and decorate with a slice of orange.

TRILBY COCKTAIL

2 dashes of Pernod

2 dashes of orange bitters

⅓ Parfait Amour

⅓ Scotch whisky

⅓ sweet vermouth

Shake well and strain into a cocktail glass. The original version of this cocktail contained absinthe but Pernod is now used.

TOM AND JERRY COCKTAIL

If not a classic cocktail, this is a veteran which was served in the taprooms of the United States in the nineteenth century.

1 egg

1 fl oz rum

1 fl oz brandy

1 tablespoon confectioners' sugar

Beat the yolk and white of the egg separately, then mix together. Use a stem glass or a china mug; add the liquor and sugar, fill up with boiling water and grate nutmeg on top.

WHITE LADY

¼ fresh lemon juice

¼ Cointreau

½ dry gin

Shake well and strain into a cocktail glass, in which a maraschino cherry has been placed.

AFTER-DINNER COCKTAILS

BLACK RUSSIAN

⅔ vodka

⅓ Kahlúa

Layer in an ice-filled old-fashioned glass.

BRANDY ALEXANDER

⅓ Crème de Cacao

⅓ brandy

⅓ heavy cream

Shake well and strain into a cocktail glass.

GODFATHER

1½ fl oz vodka

¾ fl oz Amaretto

Layer in an ice-filled old-fashioned glass.

GOLDEN CADILLAC

1 fl oz Galliano

1 fl oz white Crème de Cacao

1 fl oz heavy cream

Shake and strain into a cocktail glass.

GRASSHOPPER

⅓ white Crème de Cacao

⅓ green Crème de Menthe

⅓ heavy cream

Shake and strain into a cocktail glass.

RUSTY NAIL

½ Scotch whisky

½ Drambuie

Stir well and strain into a cocktail glass. This cocktail can also be served on the rocks.

SAVOY COCKTAIL

⅓ Crème de Cacao

⅓ Bénédictine

⅓ brandy

Use a liqueur glass and layer the ingredients carefully so they do not mix.

STINGER

¼ white Crème de Menthe

¾ brandy

Shake well and strain into a cocktail glass.

UNION JACK

⅓ Grenadine

⅓ Maraschino

⅓ green Chartreuse

Use a liqueur glass and layer the ingredients carefully so they do not mix.

WHITE RUSSIAN

⅓ vodka

⅓ Kahlúa

⅓ heavy cream

Layer in an ice-filled old-fashioned glass.

Left to right GRAND ROYAL; PLANTER'S PUNCH; GIN DAISY; MOSCOW MULE; BRANDY FIX

NON-ALCOHOLIC COCKTAILS

LONG BOAT

2 fl oz lime juice cordial
2 cubes of ice

Serve in a tall tumbler, topped up with ginger beer. Decorate with a sprig of fresh mint.

Ginger beer is a fermented drink which includes ground ginger, lemon and sugar. If unavailable, substitute ginger ale.

PUSSY FOOT

⅓ fresh orange juice
⅓ fresh lemon juice
⅓ fresh lime juice
dash of Grenadine
1 egg yolk

Shake and strain into a medium-sized glass. Add a maraschino cherry, a slice of orange and a splash of soda water.

TONGA COCKTAIL

½ fresh lemon juice
½ fresh pineapple juice
1 teaspoon Grenadine
1 egg white

Shake well and pour into a long-stemmed glass. Add a cube of ice and fill with lemonade. Decorate with a maraschino cherry and a slice of orange.

COOLERS

APRICOT COOLER

juice of ½ lemon or 1 lime
2 dashes of Grenadine
1 fl oz apricot brandy

Shake well, strain into a tall tumbler and fill with soda water.

MOSCOW MULE

2 fl oz vodka
1 dash of fresh lime juice
2 cubes of ice

Serve in a tall tumbler and fill with ginger beer. Decorate with a slice of lime and a sprig of fresh mint.

PLANTER'S PUNCH

1 fl oz fresh lemon or lime juice
½ fl oz gomme syrup
1 dash of Angostura bitters
2 fl oz Jamaica rum

Shake; pour unstrained into a tall tumbler, add a slice of pineapple, a slice of orange and a maraschino cherry. Serve with straws.

TOM COLLINS

juice of ½ lemon
1½ teaspoons confectioners' sugar
2 fl oz dry gin

Shake well and strain into a tall tumbler. Add a cube of ice and top up with soda water.

DAISIES

GIN DAISY

juice of ½ lemon
¾ teaspoon confectioners' sugar
6 dashes of Grenadine
2 fl oz gin

Use a tall tumbler. Half fill with cracked ice and stir until the glass is frosted. Fill with soda water, put 4 sprigs of fresh mint on top and decorate with slices of fruit.

WHISKEY DAISY

3 dashes of gomme syrup
juice of ½ small lemon
2 fl oz bourbon or rye whiskey

Fill a cocktail shaker one-third full with shaved ice. Shake thoroughly, strain into a small tumbler and fill up with sparkling mineral water.

FIXES

In making Fixes be careful to put the lemon peel in the glass.

BRANDY FIX

1 teaspoon sugar dissolved in 1 teaspoon water
juice of ½ lemon
½ fl oz cherry brandy
1 fl oz brandy

Frost the rim of a small tumbler with sugar. Pour the ingredients into the glass and fill with crushed ice. Stir slowly. Decorate with a slice of orange and a maraschino cherry. Serve with straws.

SANTA CRUZ FIX

1 tablespoon sugar
¼ lemon
1 fl oz water
2 fl oz rum

Pour into a small tumbler and fill two-thirds full with shaved ice. Stir with a spoon and decorate with fresh fruit.

FIZZES

BUCKS FIZZ

Put ½ fl oz fresh orange juice in a wine glass and fill with Champagne.

DERBY FIZZ

Named after the world-famous race run at Epsom, England, in summer and traditionally celebrated at the Savoy with lavish parties.

5 dashes of fresh lemon juice
1 teaspoon confectioners' sugar
1 egg
2 fl oz rye or Scotch whisky
3 dashes of Curaçao

Shake well, strain into a medium-sized glass and fill with soda water.

Left to right   EGG SOUR; HORSE'S NECK; PINEAPPLE JULEP; SAVOY RICKEY; SINGAPORE SLING

GRAND ROYAL FIZZ

juice of ½ lemon

1½ teaspoons confectioners' sugar

2 fl oz gin

2 dashes of Maraschino

juice of ¼ orange

1 tablespoon heavy cream

Shake well, strain into a medium-sized glass and fill with soda water.

HIGHBALLS

HORSE'S NECK

1½ fl oz brandy

2 dashes of Angostura bitters

2 cubes of ice

Use a tall tumbler and fill with ginger ale. Peel the rind of a lemon spirally in one piece and place one end over the edge of the tumbler, allowing the remainder to curl inside.

SPRITZER

½ dry white wine

½ soda water

Pour into a large ice-filled glass. Add a twist of lemon.

JULEPS

"One of the most delightful and insinuating potations that ever was invented," the English novelist Captain Marryat RN wrote in his diary while traveling through the southern United States in 1838. It was he who introduced the beverage to the British Isles.

PINEAPPLE JULEP (for 6 people)

juice of 2 oranges

2 fl oz raspberry vinegar

2 fl oz Maraschino

3 fl oz gin

1 bottle of sparkling Moselle or Saumur wine

Fill a large glass jug quarter-full with crushed ice. Pour in the ingredients. Pull a pineapple to pieces with a silver fork and place the pieces in the jug. Stir the mixture and decorate with a little fresh fruit.

SOUTHERN MINT JULEP

4 sprigs of fresh mint

1½ teaspoons confectioners' sugar

2 fl oz bourbon or rye whiskey

Use a tall tumbler and crush the mint leaves and confectioners' sugar together lightly. Add the whiskey and fill the glass with cracked ice. Stir gently until the glass is frosted. Decorate with 3 sprigs of fresh mint.

RICKEYS

Rickeys can be made with any liquor or liqueur. Put 2 fl oz of the chosen liquor or liqueur, the juice of ½ lime or ¼ lemon and a cube of ice in a medium-sized glass, and top up with carbonated water.

SAVOY RICKEY

1 cube of ice

juice of ½ lime or ¼ lemon

2 fl oz gin

4 dashes of Grenadine

Fill with carbonated water and leave the peel of lime or lemon in the glass.

SLINGS

GIN SLING

1 teaspoon sugar dissolved in water

2 fl oz dry gin

1 cube of ice

Serve in a tall tumbler and fill with water or soda water. It can be served hot with a little nutmeg grated on top.

SINGAPORE SLING

juice of ¼ lemon

⅔ dry gin

⅓ cherry brandy

Shake well, strain into a medium-sized glass and fill with soda water. Add a cube of ice.

SOURS

A sour is usually prepared from the following recipe:

juice of ½ lemon

1 teaspoon sugar

2 fl oz liquor or liqueur

Shake well and strain into a medium-sized glass. Add a squirt of soda water and a slice of orange with a maraschino cherry.

EGG SOUR

1 teaspoon confectioners' sugar

2 dashes of fresh lemon juice

1 fl oz Curaçao

1 fl oz brandy

1 egg

2–3 small cubes of ice

Shake well and remove the ice before serving.

ACKNOWLEDGEMENTS

Special thanks to Ian Coleman, Giorgio Locatelli, Ian Moore, David Sharland
and Peter Dorelli for their help in the preparation of this book.

INDEX